MAKING SENSE OF MODI'S INDIA

MAKING SENSE OF MODI'S INDIA

Meghnad Desai * Gyanendra Pandey
* Shruti Kapila * Radhika Desai
* R. Jagannathan * Faisal Devji
* Beena Sarwar * Sudheendra Kulkarni
* Zoya Hasan * V. Krishna Ananth
* Andrew Whitehead * Sevanti Ninan
* Rashmee Roshan Lall

HarperCollins *Publishers* India

First published in hardback in India in 2016 by
HarperCollins *Publishers* India

Anthology and introduction copyright © HarperCollins *Publishers* India 2016
Copyright for individual pieces vests with the authors

P-ISBN: 978-93-5177-632-1
E-ISBN:978-93-5177-633-8

2 4 6 8 10 9 7 5 3 1

HarperCollins *Publishers*
A-75, Sector 57, Noida, Uttar Pradesh 201301, India
1 London Bridge Street, London, SE1 9GF, United Kingdom
Hazelton Lanes, 55 Avenue Road, Suite 2900, Toronto, Ontario M5R 3L2
and 1995 Markham Road, Scarborough, Ontario M1B 5M8, Canada
25 Ryde Road, Pymble, Sydney, NSW 2073, Australia
195 Broadway, New York, NY 10007. USA

Typeset in 11.5/15 Garamond Premier Pro
By Saanvi Graphics Noida

Printed and bound at
Replika Press Pvt. Ltd.

Contents

Introduction

In a few months, Narendra Modi will have completed two years
in office. Vowing to build a 'new' India, he came to power with
a massive mandate after a bitterly fought election in May 2014.
His idea of an India ideologically and culturally different from
the post-independent Nehruvian one has been endlessly debated.
But it remains a big conundrum with no clarity as to what his big
alternative vision is.

So, where's India headed under Modi?

For an answer, it is important, first, to grasp the profound meaning of
the 2014 verdict, which, many believe, has not been fully understood.
It is true that at one level the vote was against a bumbling, 'corrupt' and
leaderless Congress, but at a deeper level it was also a comprehensive
repudiation of the concept of a benign, tolerant and liberal India
in favour of a majoritarian and economically laissez-faire nation
unencumbered by 'soft' Nehruvian baggage. But nearly two years later,
the country remains precariously poised at a point where, having voted
for a decisive break with the past, it is still waiting expectantly to be led
to the new promised land.

There's growing scepticism as to whether Modi really has a new long-
term vision; whether the talk of a 'new' India is simply a sales pitch. As

a slogan, 'new' India has a nice ring, but slogans, however seductive, are no substitute for a philosophical vision.

This book is an attempt, with the help of Modi's supporters and critics alike, to analyse the Modi 'phenomenon', the factors behind it, and what it means for the future of India. Such a debate is important at a time when there are deep and legitimate concerns about the future of secularism amid calls for a redefinition of traditional notions of nationhood.

ISSUES AT STAKE

Here is a flavour of the issues raised in this volume.

Meghnad Desai draws on the history of European nationalism to analyse the nature of Hindu nationalist resurgence. And though a supporter of Modi's 'development' pledge, he shares concerns about his Hindutva baggage. R. Jagannathan, also a Modi supporter, tries to figure out his vision and what he represents. Is Modi really the man we see on the tin? 'What is he like as a person as opposed to his airbrushed image? What does he really believe in as opposed to what he has said after becoming prime minister of India? What is his economics about?' he asks. His answers to these and a series of other questions he raises add up to an intriguing portrait of a man who remains an enigma as much to his critics as to his admirers.

Gyanendra Pandey examines Modi's development agenda in the light of the new global fashion that insists on development, 'sought at times *in spite* of the people, often against the interests of the poor and unprivileged: working people, the underemployed and unemployed'. And he worries that this development model is now being sought to be imposed on India's poor and marginalized sections, which are presented as 'backward' and 'primitive' and which 'must be drawn into "our" time – the time of development – however great the cost'.

Making sense of the 'real' character of the RSS has been one of the most hotly debated issues of our time; and it has assumed a new urgency in view of Modi's RSS roots and the perception that his government is being remote-controlled by Mohan Bhagwat. The RSS's insistence that it is simply a social and cultural organization with no political agenda has long been questioned, but there is no consensus on the real nature of the beast, with the academia and the commentariat deeply divided over whether it can be characterized as a fascist organization.

In a trenchant analysis, Radhika Desai declares her impatience with the 'ifs' and 'buts' that have tended to characterize the debate and what she calls the 'tediously earnest discussions of the founding ideas of the Hindutva ideologues' that have prevented academics such as Christophe Jaffrelot from designating the RSS as a fascist organization. Drawing on the history of European fascism and her own close study of the RSS doctrine and its pattern of behaviour, she has no doubt that it is fascist in tooth and claw. The entire Sangh Parivar, including the BJP, represents well-recognized 'fascist' tendencies dressed up in democratic posturing, she argues.

Faisal Devji casts a critical eye on the secularism-versus-communalism debate in which a 'secular' Congress and 'communal' BJP are portrayed as representing the opposite ends of Indian politics. He finds such a discourse 'too superficial' and unhelpful in understanding the nature of Indian polity, which is often marked by 'greater continuity between parties ... than is usually recognized to be the case'. It is in the light of such 'continuities' that he analyses the implications of the Modi victory and throws up some intriguing questions.

Zoya Hasan looks at the causes and implications of the Congress collapse and warns that any attempt by the Congress leadership to 'reshape itself as pale saffron in a bid to mimic the winner will only help to legitimize the right-wing political discourse, while failing to pick up the electoral dividends from this competitive wooing of the Hindu vote'. Krishna Ananth, in his critique of the decline of the Left, calls for a root-and-branch overhaul of its blinkered ideological programme and flawed tactics if it is serious about making itself relevant again in national politics.

Shruti Kapila warns that the personality cult being sought to be built around Modi, which, far from making any attempt to discourage, he is actively promoting, could come to haunt the BJP besides producing 'unforeseen consequences' for Indian democracy. Sudheendra Kulkarni, a former BJP activist who knows the Sangh Parivar inside out, warns against its 'anti-Muslim and anti-minorities propaganda' and criticizes Modi for not reining it in. But, ultimately, he believes that compulsions of power and Modi's political instincts for survival would force him to 'distance' his government from such elements and 'actively curb' them. 'Modi is an astute politician and he knows that alienating a large section of the Indian population would create problems for his premiership – especially for his desire to win a second term in 2019,' he writes.

But will he?

The role of the media, owned by big corporates, in promoting Modi has come under close scrutiny. There is a perception that, to use L.K. Advani's memorable phrase from the Emergency, the media seems only too eager to 'crawl' when 'asked to simply bend'.

But Sevanti Ninan, one of India's more sober media commentators, has a more nuanced take on it. She questions the 'catch-all' media label used to describe 'a technologically diverse universe of communication', and the tendency, then, to ascribe to it 'a common behaviour pattern ... as in, the media is turning right, or turning saffron, or enabling the ascent of Narendra Modi'. 'But is there a pattern, and is it consistent?' she asks in a closely argued analysis of the rapidly changing complexion of the Indian media. She finds much of the debate too simplistic which, according to her, ignores an understanding of the increasingly complex media environment.

Modi's forays into foreign policy and his bid to raise India's profile in the international arena have impressed many, but he has also been accused of using foreign policy to project India as a 'Hindu power' with his nationalistic – 'Hindu pride' – narrative, especially in his pitch to Indian expats abroad. Andrew Whitehead, a former BBC (British Broadcasting Corporation) correspondent in Delhi, offers an insight into how the West views the new Indian prime minister. Modi, he says, has 'got off to a good start' and is seen in most Western capitals as a leader who 'wants to strike a new, more positive note in his country's engagement with Western powers' and 'needs to be met halfway'. But this is combined with 'an anxiety about the BJP's at times stridently assertive religion-based nationalism'. 'If Barack Obama has delivered the choicest of tributes, he has also voiced anxieties about communal tension and violence in India,' he writes, alluding to the US President's remarks on his visit to India in January 2015 on the Sangh Parivar's hate campaigns against Muslims and Christians.

Finally, what is the view from across the border in Pakistan? And what do Indian expats other than Modi's supporters in Manhattan and Wembley make of the 'new' India in the making? Beena Sarwar and Rashmee Roshan Lall provide refreshingly candid perspectives that might make interesting reading for many newly nationalist Indians.

Arguably, independent India has seldom been as politically and culturally polarized as it is today. Recent months have seen an alarming rise in hate speech, shrill Hindu nationalistic rhetoric, attacks on dissenting writers and academics (renowned rationalist thinker M.M. Kalburgi was shot dead for his views on idol worship and Hindu rituals, prompting many eminent writers to return their Sahitya Akademi awards) and controversies around beef eating and 'Hindu sensitivities'.

Clearly, the emerging face of Modi's 'new' India is not looking pretty. Maybe it is a passing phase; but at the moment it is hard to be too optimistic.

Over to the debate.

India as a Hindu Nation – and Other Ideas of India

Meghnad Desai

꧁

Meghnad Desai is emeritus professor of economics at the London School of Economics and author of *The Rediscovery of India* and *Development and Nationhood*.

The Bharatiya Janata Party's triumph in the 2014 general elections, securing a majority in the Lok Sabha on its own (a 'first' for any party since 1984), was an event of transformational significance. Narendra Modi has changed expectations about India and generated a new mood of optimism. But, given his RSS background and BJP's political proclivities, it is very likely that during his rule the old idea of India – the Nehruvian idea of secular India which has been hegemonic so far – will be challenged. It is early to say what precise form this will take. But it is, perhaps, time to open up the debate around the idea of India's nationhood. What makes India a nation?

THE IDEA OF A NATION

The idea of nationhood is of recent origin. One can date it from sometime after the French Revolution. Johann Gottfried von Herder, the nineteenth-century German philosopher, was the first to explicitly speak of a nation as a 'folk' or a homogeneous community. Debates since then have raged as to what constitutes a nation, and what is the explanation for nationalism's appeal.

Its origin and appeal have invited many explanations from scholars. Just to take three of my former London School of Economics (LSE) colleagues who wrote on nationalism. Ernest Gellner, hailed as one of the most 'vigorous' European intellectuals of his time, argued that nationalism is a product of modernity and industrial capitalism. Historian Elie Kedourie, a trenchant critic of British support for Arab nationalism, thought of nationalism as a dangerous epidemic which has done untold harm to the world. Anthony Smith, regarded as one of the pioneers of 'nationalism studies', holds the view that a nation has to have primordial roots to be a nation.

A nation can be defined by a common language, a religion, a racial or ethnic identity and a common history. A nation has to have the idea that it is timeless. Its origins have to be in the distant past and if the nation is a subject nation at the moment of fashioning its identity, there has to be the notion that at the beginning was a 'golden age' from which the nation has declined to its present plight. But the idea requires nationalists to believe that the nation will rise again and become powerful.

Hindu Mahasabha leader Vinayak Damodar Savarkar (popularly known as Veer Savarkar), who coined the term Hindutva, was the first Hindu nationalist to characterize the events of 1857 as the Indian War of Independence. But the fact is that the 1857 rebels did not so much fight for an Indian nation as for restoration of the Mughal Empire. The rebellion of 1857 was confined very much to what later came to be dubbed BIMARU states comprising Bihar, Madhya Pradesh,

Rajasthan and Uttar Pradesh. Punjab, Bombay (then the capital of Bombay Presidency), and much of south India remained uninvolved though scattered local revolts have since been documented and are much prized. It was after the collapse of the 1857 rebellion that the idea of India as a nation with its destiny independent of any past kingdom or Empire took shape.

As a latecomer to the arena of nations, India faced special problems defining its nationhood. National consciousness began to appear in the nineteenth century among the products of recently introduced Western education. Thus, the first characteristic of the Indian idea of a nation was that it was reactive to foreign rule.

During the second half of the nineteenth century, for the first time in its long history, India was united in a single administrative entity – British India. It was then that India's borders were determined. This is why India's borders, both before and after its Partition in 1947, have British names: Durand Line, McMahon Line and Radcliffe Line. British India was bound together by an administrative iron frame, a rail network and a postal and telegraph system. The many princely states were beholden to the British viceroy in a paramountcy arrangement. The three Presidency centres of Bombay, Calcutta and Madras were centres of recruitment of the elite who would shape the various ideas of India. The task of the first generation of nationalists was easy. The unity of Indians was defined by a common enemy, the British. At the time, though, they did not imagine themselves as an independent nation. They demanded to be treated as much as possible on par with other subjects of the Crown as Victoria's Declaration, hailed as Magna Carta of India by Surendranath Banerjea, a distinguished progressive political leader, had promised.

Here began the first of the many fissures of the definition of Indian nationhood. Who were they demanding the rights for, and why did they deserve them? The westernized elite argued that they had imbibed the best of British values of conservative Edmund Burke and libertarian

John Stuart Mill, and thus qualified as well-educated subjects to compete for public service.

But there was another strand which wanted to restore Indian pride in the face of British attempts, especially by the clergy, to humiliate them, which included denigrating their religion. This led to a movement to revive and reform Hindu religion. Dayanand Saraswati, the founder of the Arya Samaj, favoured going back to the Vedic roots of Hinduism. Rammohun Roy's Brahmo Samaj, on the other hand, opted for a Unitarian Church–style monotheistic model for reforming Hinduism. Swami Vivekananda, revered as the 'patriotic saint', is credited with introducing Hinduism to the world – stressing the message of the Upanishads. The differences between Gopal Krishna Gokhale and Bal Gangadhar Tilak, leading figures in the freedom movement, illustrate two rival approaches to Indian nationhood at the turn of the twentieth century.

ISLAM–CHRISTIANITY DIVIDE

Unlike their relationship with Hindus, the British had a more complicated relationship with Muslims. The antagonism between Christians and Muslims had existed since the Crusades, if not before that. In Europe, the threat of the Ottoman Empire remained potent till the Battle of Lepanto when a coalition of southern European Catholic states defeated its forces on 7 October 1571. Yet, things were changing. Just before 1857, the British had gone to the aid of the Ottoman Empire to fight the Russian threat in the Crimean War. Even so, the fright that 1857 gave to the British was blamed on Muslims.

The first cautious Muslim overture to the British to recover from the humiliation caused by the collapse of the rebellion was made by Sir Syed Ahmad Khan, the nineteenth-century philosopher and social reformer who later founded Aligarh Muslim University (AMU) to promote Western-style modern education among Muslims. Like the westernized Hindu and Parsi elite, he wanted Muslims to remain loyal to the British and exercise patience in dealing with them. As a modernizer, he kept his appeal free from any hint of Islamic revivalism. But there was also a more combative strand of religious opposition to British rule represented by the Deoband and the Barelvi religious establishments. They did not want any accommodation by way of jobs or favours. They also did not subscribe to the idea of a nation but only of the Dar al-Islam (literally meaning, house or abode of peace) as a whole.

The British never defined themselves as a nation but as loyal subjects of a kingdom divided by class and religion. They viewed India and, indeed, their other colonies in the same way. In the first concessions to Indian loyalists' demand for a say in governance, they granted limited representation to a certain class of citizens under the Indian Councils Act of 1909 but, at the same time, they created a special dispensation for Muslims, causing further hiatus in Hindu–Muslim relations. However, at the historic joint session of the Congress and Muslim League in Lucknow in 1916, Muhammad Ali Jinnah, who was a member of both parties, succeeded in reconciling their differences on the issue through what is known as the 'Lucknow Pact', earning him the title of 'the ambassador of Hindu–Muslim Unity' courtesy Sarojini Naidu.

GANDHI'S APPROACH

Gandhi had begun as a loyalist of the British Empire and argued his case for the rights of indentured workers in South Africa on the basis of Victoria's Declaration. It was after Jallianwala Bagh that he changed his stance. He launched the Khilafat movement which brought together Muslims and Hindus under one umbrella to argue for redressing Muslim grievances while mobilizing Hindus with the promise of Swaraj within one year. Rejecting the 1919 government proposals aimed at expanding Indian participation in the colonial administration – a follow-up to the 1909 reforms – Gandhi launched a non-violent non-cooperation movement. But after a violent incident in Chauri Chaura, Uttar Pradesh, in 1922, he suspended the movement despite having failed to deliver on his promise.

From then on, Muslims became antagonistic towards Gandhi and the Congress. Only a tiny minority of 'nationalist Muslims' remained with the Congress. The Lucknow Pact was dead, and Jinnah left the Congress.

Gandhi preached an ecumenical approach to politics and waged his battles with the British using a religious idiom. He forged a consensus between the Gokhale and Tilak approaches – modern liberal and constitutional but imbued with a religious idiom. Gandhi's Hinduism was milder than Tilak's. His goal was to drive the British out with a mass movement led by the Congress. Congress insisted on its hegemony as the only party the British should negotiate with. The British ignored this demand and legislated the Government of India Act of 1935 which was to lead to Dominion status. There was no agreement, however, on reconciling Hindu–Muslim differences. When elections were held in 1937, the idea of Congress hegemony suffered a huge blow. The Congress failed to win Muslim seats though the Muslim League did not do well either. In the 1946 elections, the Muslim League won almost all the Muslim seats across India. The final result after ten years of many British missions and parleys was the Partition of British India into two entities, India and Pakistan.

CRISIS OF INDIAN NATIONHOOD

Until 1947, the idea of India that was promoted was aimed at maintaining the unity of undivided India. Jawaharlal Nehru's *The Discovery of India* is the final and the best history of the Indian nation as it never became. The crisis of Indian nationhood began with the country's Partition. For, clearly, the India of which Nehru had become prime minister was not the India he had imagined. And this remains the unsettled question of Indian nationhood. Nehru proposed a theory of nationhood which ignored the Partition altogether, seeing India instead as a continuing story as though nothing had changed. He still saw it as a nation in which Hindus, Muslims and all other religious communities lived happily ever after.

This, what I would call the wishful forgetfulness of the reality of Partition, lies at the heart of our present debate. Jinnah had argued that there were two 'nations' within British India. He won the argument and got his wish. But what he got was a nation state with a Muslim majority – not the entire so-called 'Muslim nation' he had wished for as a large number of Muslims chose to remain in India. The Congress conceded Partition but kept denying that it had accepted the two-nation theory. By his forceful advocacy and the Congress hegemony in elections, Nehru institutionalized his idea of India as a nation. An entire edifice–intellectual, cultural, political – was constructed around this 'Idea of India' as a secular democratic country.

This idea remained dominant while Nehru ruled and even through the first phase of Indira Gandhi's rule, the thirty years between 1947 and 1977. But it began to be questioned with the rise of Hindu nationalism in the 1980s. The Jana Sangh, later renamed the Bharatiya Janata Party, acquired wider acceptability after it joined leading mainstream parties to oppose Indira Gandhi's dictatorial Emergency in 1975. The Emergency exposed the democratic liberal credentials of the Congress and made it vulnerable to attacks. The BJP chose to target its secularism, and began to question the post-Partition idea of India. If there were two 'nations', and if one (Muslim) 'nation' had got Pakistan, what about the other (Hindu) 'nation'? Why was India not a Hindu nation to counter the Muslim nation that Pakistan was? Why did Muslims get help to go on pilgrimage to Mecca but not Hindus to Haridwar or Rameshwaram?

This Hindu nationalist argument was not countered seriously and, instead, dismissed as an obscurantist and divisive viewpoint. India, it was argued, must remain secular and eschew an exclusivist Hindu identity in the interest of communal peace and harmony. The secular idea was underpinned by a reading of Indian history which lionized 'good secular' kings – Ashoka and Akbar being the only two who passed muster. Hinduism was downplayed even by Hindu politicians while Muslim festivals became a political tool to bolster Indian secularism.

It was never a satisfactory intellectual exercise despite the exclusive patronage it received in universities and research centres. The argument began to lose traction as soon as the Congress lost its majority in Parliament in 1989. Until then, while the Congress elite had benefited from English education and exposure to the outside world that came with foreign travels, its more home-grown rivals had to make do with substandard local education. But with economic liberalization, it became easier to go abroad. The Indian diaspora is mainly Hindu, and in the USA and the UK it began to assert its support for the alternative idea of India – the idea of a Hindu India–propelling the BJP to power as a majority party after many years and bringing to the fore the 'other' Idea of India. But what is it? Is it coherent? Is it sustainable as an idea of nationhood?

TWO SIDES OF NARENDRA MODI

Narendra Modi was the first BJP leader to work out from his perch in Gujarat that an exclusively religious nationalism is not a winning formula. Between 1989 and 2014, even as the Congress struggled to regain a majority, the BJP failed to make much headway – never exceeding 182 seats, about a third of the total. Modi's 2014 campaign marked a departure from all previous BJP campaigns. It offered a forward-looking aspirational vision of development in which every Indian regardless of religion could gain. He went to areas long neglected, and fashioned a strategy which was tech-savvy and gave a promise of harnessing the latest technology from around the world to raise India's economic profile. He downplayed BJP's Hindu nationalist message. When he did perform his ritual worship of the Ganga, he talked as much about cleaning it up as about its holiness. He has talked of cleaning up India as an unfulfilled dream of Gandhi. On 15 August 2014, he projected a unifying vision of India.

The rest of the BJP and RSS go along only partly with Modi's vision. They see the party's massive victory as the beginning of a campaign of cultural war to redefine India as a Hindu nation. They are impatient to establish their stations along the way which they hope will defeat the Congress vision of India once and for all. This culture war will be fought by influencing policies of key ministries. Whether Modi is orchestrating these moves is not certain. It may even be that if such tactics become expensive in terms of winning elections, he may put a stop to this. (He did not support the BJP candidates in the 2014 UP by-elections where the BJP candidates were openly anti-secular and lost.) Leaving that aside, let me examine the content of Hindu nationalism.

BASIC PROPOSITIONS OF HINDU NATIONALISM

The following propositions are at the core of the Hindu nationalist doctrine:

(1) India has always been a single nation since prehistoric times as Bharatavarsha or Aryabhoomi.

(2) India got enslaved when Muslim invaders came from the north-west from the eighth century onwards – Mohammad Bin Qaseem and then Mahmud Gazni followed by the Delhi Sultanate and then the Mughal Empire. Muslims are foreigners. The corollary of this xenophobia is to deny that the Aryans came to India from elsewhere. There is a tension about reconciling the Indus Valley culture with the story of Aryan incursions. The Hindu nationalists deny point-blank that Aryans were foreigners.

(3) The British did not create a single Indian entity. It was always there. The education which Macaulay introduced created the elite – Macaulay-putras – who behave and think like foreigners.

(4) In 1947, 1,200 years of slavery came to an end. (Narendra Modi said as much during his first speech in the Central Hall

of Parliament after his election.) India was at last free to assert its true identity as a Hindu nation.

(5) Congress secularists, however, went on privileging Muslims whose loyalty is always to be doubted as their nation is Pakistan.

These propositions raise several conceptual and historical issues. Let's examine them.

First, there is the issue of the native versus the foreigner. The British were clearly foreigners. They came when they had a job to do and never settled in India or 'colonized' it as they did Rhodesia or Australia. Muslims emperors, on the other hand, did not go back and made India their home. This creates a problem for the Hindu nationalist. For him, the fact that they have been here for 1,200 years does not make them natives of India. They shall forever remain alien. This is a strange doctrine because India was the receptacle for many 'foreign' tribes throughout its history – the Shakas, the Huns, the Scythians and many other 'races', all of whom converted to Hinduism. But, then, 1,200 years are not enough. What about the Aryans? Did the Aryans also not come from central Europe or the Arctic, as Tilak argued?

To say that the Aryans are foreigners would make Hinduism a foreign religion. The aborigines – tribals – would then be the only true natives, as some Dalit scholars have argued. That is why Hindu nationalists deny foreign origin of the Aryans. The Aryans have to be primordially native to suit the Hindu nationalist narrative which imagines a time when somehow instantaneously Hinduism was established across all of India thanks to the Vedas and the Brahmins performing sacrifices, etc. Sanskrit has to have the prime place as lingua franca of Hindu India for that reason.

This is the stuff of bogus history. The religion which Hindus practise has only a marginal relationship to the Vedas. The Vedic gods are no longer worshipped. Vishnu, Shiva and Kali appear in the Hindu pantheon at least 1,000 years after the Vedas. The slow spread of Brahmanism (as the religion should be properly called) from its Punjab heartland to Delhi region and then on to UP and Bihar has been well charted. The importance of Pali and Ardhamagadhi in the propagation of Ajivikas, Jainism and Buddhism from the sixth century BCE onwards is also known.

It took a thousand-year struggle between Buddhism and Brahmanism before the latter could declare a complete victory. India became a Hindu nation about the time the Adi Shankaracharya debated and defeated the Buddhists. If the chronology of Hindu nationalists is taken seriously, however, it should be soon after India became 'slave' to Muslims.

The Hindu nationalist strategy is to deny any conflict between Buddhism and Brahmanism and claim that Buddha was an avatar of Vishnu. This assertion is not found till the seventh century CE in the Puranas, by which time Buddhism was on its way out. Hinduism is not enough to define India as a Hindu nation throughout its history.

Savarkar tried to square this circle in his essay on Hindutva. He was a modernist and not a devotee of religion. His idea of nation is derived from the then fashionable ideas of nationhood espoused by the newly born nations of Europe, many of them parts of the Habsburg Empire which broke up in 1918 – Hungary, Poland, Czechoslovakia. Nationhood depended on territory and those born in the territory were members of the nation. His Hindutva is not tied to Hinduism. It says that anyone born in the land of the Indus–Sindhu is a Hindu and part of Hindutva. There is a subtext that Hindus are more so than Muslims. But Muslims can belong to Hindutva if they are loyal to the land of their birth. Subsequent Hindu nationalists have adopted the notion of Hindutva but not Savarkar's secular doctrine.

As a history of India, the Hindu nationalist story is as partial as the story that the Nehruvian vision has created. Of course, they are both north India–biased stories. They take Delhi and its rulers to be all of India. Muslim raiders may have come in the eighth century to Sind and

Saurashtra and in the twelfth century established the Delhi Sultanate. But they never penetrated south of the Vindhyas. South India has a very different history about Muslim immigrants from that of north India. Nor did it 'suffer' from Muslim rule till very late when Aurangzeb went to south in late seventeenth century. Hindu kingdoms were coexistent with Muslim ones in the south but that happened only in the middle of the second millennium. The whole idea of '1,200 years of slavery' is spurious. Assam was never conquered by any Muslim power.

But ultimately there will never be 'true objective' history. There never is in any nation. Debates and reinterpretations go on forever. Patronage to academia can be used to commission histories to buttress the official line. The sanctity of dispassionate research can never be guaranteed if the funding is public. India, however, does not have the tradition of private philanthropy for research. The government guards all the doors to higher education, thanks to the statist bias of the Congress which ruled for the first thirty years uninterruptedly. This bias has permeated the BJP as well.

It is not the idea of Hindu nationalism that is worrying. It is that the government will be the propagator of this particular view. What are the prospects?

PECULIARITIES OF HINDU SOCIETY AND RELIGION

The one consolation we have is that Hinduism is unlike any other religion. Indeed, when Christians came to India, they asked for Hindus' Holy Book. Instead of saying that is not our way; we have scores of holy books, Hindus rushed to name the Vedas as the Holy Book. Now, it is the Bhagavad Gita which is supposedly the Holy Book. But Hinduism has no creed. It is not monotheistic. It can be polytheistic, or non-deist in its concept of the Brahman. It has several gods and multiple forms of worship. Hindus are not a single Church. They are not united.

The Hindu nationalist knows this. There was a systematic attempt to semitize Hinduism by launching the Ramjanmabhoomi movement which led to the demolition of the Babri Masjid, a sixteenth-century mosque in Ayodhya (UP), in 1992. But soon the BJP realized that this was not a unifying strategy and failed to earn any political dividends from it. Atal Bihari Vajpayee, when he became prime minister, quietly abandoned the temple issue; and Narendra Modi has not revived it. Hindu nationalism remains largely a north Indian phenomenon and failed to win many adherents in the south. Ideas of Aryabhoomi and Sanskrit dominance are not likely to be popular in the south. This was seen in DMK leader M. Karunanidhi's reaction to the claim that Rama Setu was a historical fact rather than a myth. (In the Ramayana, Rama Setu features as a bridge that an army of Vanar [monkeys] built for Lord Rama to reach Lanka and rescue Sita from Ravana's captivity.)

Whatever the religion, Hindu society is by its very nature hierarchical and inegalitarian. The traditionalists can deny that the caste system was always as it is now but they cannot deny the inequalities of status among the Hindus. The Dalit movement has made it clear that they do not buy the claim that Hinduism is all-encompassing. Hindus are not a single people; either by belief or by status.

Narendra Modi is well aware of this. Many in the BJP are conservative Hindus who believe in the sanctity of caste and the divine sanction for it, as in the Bhagavad Gita, but an OBC (Other Backward Classes, a category of lower castes), Modi, has experienced the disadvantages of low-caste status. He articulates a unifying vision for all Indians. He may even become a radical social reformer as far as caste is concerned, but the rest of the BJP will abandon him if he does.

But that is to be too sanguine. The possibility of a different vision of India is very palpable and we have to think of its likely consequences.

WHO IS AFRAID OF RELIGION?

Not all modern nations are secular. In the United Kingdom, the head of the state has to be an Anglican. He/she is also head of the Church of England. But it is a secular society, and the state guarantees human rights to all its subjects regardless of religion. But this freedom was achieved quite painstakingly through the nineteenth and twentieth centuries, first by non-Anglican Protestants – the non-conformists – then the Catholics and finally the Jews. When a large wave of immigrants arrived after 1945, their religion was no barrier. It was their race which had to be overcome as a discriminatory factor by the society. This could be done because it had a robust human rights regime. The UK is a Christian nation but a tolerant one.

America, on the other hand, is a secular state but the Christian religion there is dominant. The president-elect swears on the Bible. There has never been a non-Christian president and it was not until 1961 that a Catholic became president. The currency says, 'In God we Trust.'

The issue with Hindu nationalism is not its bad history. It is the idea that it harbours the notion of two classes of citizens in which Hindus are the 'original' full members of a Hindu India while others – Christians, Muslims, Parsis – are on sufferance of the majority. India has given itself a modern liberal Constitution with Fundamental Rights to all its citizens. It should not matter how the nation describes itself so long as these rights are guaranteed to everyone.

It is here that doubts concerning the Hindu nationalist doctrine surface. What we know is that even under Nehruvian secularism, the safety and security of minorities were not guaranteed. If the law is broken and violence committed, victims find it difficult to get justice if the local authorities can be browbeaten. Muslims have difficulty renting or owning property wherever they may choose despite the law being against such bias. Hindu–Muslim riots have been frequent across India. During the past fifty years (1964–2014), there were around 15,000 communal riots in which the victims were mostly Muslims. Justice is notoriously slow and often not delivered if the ruling party is involved as a likely predator. The anti-Sikh riots of 1984 still stand as an indictment of Nehruvian secularism.

This is the principal reason for fearing Hindu nationalism. The only guarantee against its dominance will be civil society's vigilance to ensure the protection of human rights, and maintenance of the rule of law. India needs many more non-state actors and agencies to guard the interests of its citizens irrespective of their religion (or, indeed, those who profess no religion), to make sure that the state does not misuse its power to deny equal citizenship to all. It will not be an easy task. India needs a healthy dose of scepticism about the virtues of the state as a guarantor of its citizens' liberties. This is because there is no neutral state. There are only governments and they are run by politicians who belong to political parties which are all too often ploughing their own furrow.

The lesson is to beware of any one particular Idea of India which becomes hegemonic. Pluralism requires that there be many Ideas of India, not one. Finally, I offer my own Idea of India.

INDIA AS A MULTINATIONAL POLITY

India is a union of many nations, not one. Each region with its own language has a national identity. Each state has a large enough territory and distinct enough identity to qualify as a nation on its own. Each has a rich local political history. Just think of the histories of the Marathas, the Sikhs, the Rajputs, the Bengalis and the Tamils. Or the unwritten histories of the Dalits and the many tribal communities. India has never had a single political history as China has had. A hero in one nation is a villain in another. No single nation (by this definition of a cohesive linguistic regional group) has dominated India for any length of time. Delhi was never the centre of power for all of India till Rajendra Prasad became president in 1950. It was then that India became for the first time in its history a single political entity. There is a reason for this.

The British were able to defeat all other European powers first, and then Indian powers one by one between 1757 and 1857. They then consolidated their power by unifying India administratively. The leaders of the Indian independence movement imbibed the principles of liberal democracy, human rights and rule of law from their masters. They used this to fashion a Constitution for India as a sovereign democratic republic at its birth. It is this Constitution and the practice of parliamentary democracy which makes India a viable union of nations. It is this which is the guarantee of India's survival and prosperity. There should be as many Ideas of India as there are the nations within India.

A People's History of India, 1947–2014: Inclusive Development Not for All

Gyanendra Pandey

᷍ᐯ᷍

Gyanendra Pandey, a distinguished historian, founding member and leading theorist of subaltern studies, is the author most recently of *A History of Prejudice* (2013).

Nationalism, development and democracy were among the most rousing political slogans of the twentieth century. Slogans advanced on behalf of the people, the poor and downtrodden in every land: sometimes inspired and even led by them.

Nationalism, development and even democracy continue to be mouthed as political slogans today, although the balance between them has shifted to some degree. In formal speech, nationalism is somewhat at a discount: yet nationhood and democracy are assumed to be in place in any country that can hold up a national flag and stage periodic elections approved in some way by 'international observers'. Given the complacency – or, in some places, despair – with regard to these two ideas, the overriding emphasis across the globe is on development, also called economic growth. A development that is sought at times *in spite* of the people, often against the interests of the poor and unprivileged: working people, the underemployed and unemployed.

This essay has the modest aim of examining some of the implications of this shift in the context of recent happenings in India.

THE UMBRELLA OF THE NATION

An exploration of the changing conception of the reach of nationalism may usefully begin with the founding declaration of the Indian republic, adopted by the Indian Constituent Assembly on 26 November 1949: 'WE, THE PEOPLE OF INDIA, having solemnly resolved to constitute India into a SOVEREIGN DEMOCRATIC REPUBLIC and to secure to all its citizens: JUSTICE, social, economic and political; LIBERTY of thought, expression, belief, faith and worship; EQUALITY of status and of opportunity; and to promote among them all FRATERNITY assuring the dignity of the individual and the unity and integrity of the Nation; ... do hereby adopt, enact and give to ourselves this constitution.'[1]

A significant but not commonly remarked flattening is already evident in this founding document: 'We, the people of India', already a full-blown entity, speaking in one voice. It may be said that idealistic statements and expressions of political hope will inevitably be reductive, since they are couched in a language of shared sentiment and collective aspiration. It is instructive, nevertheless, to tarry a moment and consider what a more nuanced, pluralistic and processual declaration might look like. What benefits might accrue from a formulation such as the following? 'We, the *peoples* of India, with all our diverse languages, cultures, religions, hierarchies and practices (social, economic, political and intellectual), and with all the criss-crossing and fluidity and provisionality of our shared homeland and polity – having struggled to end the colonial rule of a distant power, and to gain control of our own destiny – do give to ourselves this broad and ambitious framework of rules for continued negotiation, planning and adjustment of our political, economic and cultural futures.'

Mohandas Karamchand Gandhi, the much venerated and yet much mocked Father of the Nation, who was rather less persuaded than most other political leaders of his time and since, about the verities of nationalism or the infallibility of human judgement, articulated this kind of tentative vision when asked for his definition of Swaraj, or self-rule, in 1924: 'Truthful relations between Hindus and Muslims, the removal of Untouchability, and bread for the masses. That is how I would define swaraj at the present moment.'[2] I have periodically returned to this unusual articulation, not only because of its remarkably radical character – who else but Gandhi would have, in almost Leninist fashion, brought together *peace*, *dignity* and *bread* in a definition of Indian self-rule? – but also because of its manifest provisionality: 'That is how I would define swaraj *at the present moment.*' For tomorrow, under changed conditions, with the further advance of political and social struggles, and with altered imperatives and aspirations, the needs of self-governance – freedom and dignity and collective effort – are also likely to be different.

The point about the changing resonance of a concept such as Swaraj applies just as emphatically, of course, to the historical emergence and changeability of communities and nations. These collectivities – as also individuals and families, castes and classes, and all manner of other assemblages – are constituted, and reconstituted, in continuously changing historical and political circumstances. In this respect, the self-described Indian nation began with a considerable advantage. It was not, and could hardly claim to be, a homogeneous, racially, religiously, linguistically or culturally uniform, somehow obviously defined and eternally stable nation. It has been described, on the contrary, as a multinational nation, an experiment in pluralistic living and celebration of multiplicity, not easily reduced to one book or one god, one path or one quest – even in the age of high nationalism.

The great Urdu poet Raghupati Sahai 'Firaq' put the case eloquently:

Sar zameen-i-Hind par aquaam-i-alam ke, Firaq
Qafile baste gaye, Hindostan banta gaya

(On the sacred land of Hind, caravans of nations from all over
the world
Came and settled – and Hindustan continued to evolve)

In the nineteenth and early twentieth centuries, Indian nationalist formulation, the nation and its greatness flowed from the coexistence and common struggles of these many different elements: Hindu + Muslim + Christian + Parsi + Sikh. Pandit Madan Mohan Malaviya, the distinguished lawyer, Sanskrit scholar and Hindu nationalist leader of the militantly anti-colonial Indian National Congress, whose birthday, 25 December, under the right-wing Hindu dispensation that rules India today, outshone Christmas and was celebrated along with Atal Bihari Vajpayee's as Good Governance Day, affirmed in 1905: 'Just as Hindustan [a Hindi/Urdu term for India] is the beloved birthplace of the Hindus, so it is of the Muslims too ... To establish real affection and brotherly love among these two communities and all the communities of India – Hindu, Muslim, Christian, Parsi – is the greatest duty before us all.'

Lala Lajpat Rai, another prominent leader of the Indian National Congress in the 1920s, and another luminary in the Hindu nationalist pantheon, part of the reformist Arya Samaj movement, which was at loggerheads (especially in its opposition to caste) with Malaviya's more orthodox Sanatan Dharma Hinduism, made a very similar statement in 1920: 'The Indian nation, such as it is or such as we intend to build [it], neither is nor will be exclusively Hindu, Muslim, Sikh or Christian. It will be each and all.'

Nearly a century later, in January 2014, in the course of the election campaign that brought him to power as prime minister of India,

Narendra Modi responded as follows to a question about the need for reassurance to religious minorities. Hinduism alone speaks of one truth and many paths, he declared. He went on to say that 'the official book' of Israel notes that India is the only land in which Jews were never persecuted throughout their 2,500-year history, although the text he was referring to is unclear.

It is not that the articulation of the nation in the early stages of the Indian nationalist struggle was devoid of tension, inconsistency or internal contradiction. The more public, associational strand of that movement was led to a large extent by an urban, Western-educated elite, which was predominantly upper caste and Hindu. As numerous scholars have shown, the leadership often harked back to an assumed ancient history of great Hindu philosophical and cultural achievement, and an undying tradition of accommodation of diverse cultures and practices within a peculiar caste hierarchy, as demonstrating the uniqueness and essence of India's national spirit. It was not always sensitive to the alternative traditions, beliefs and practices of India's Muslim, Christian and other religious communities, spread out all over the subcontinent, and even less concerned with the conditions and struggles of the lowest castes and classes, especially in the countryside and the remoter forest tracts – until these latter made their presence felt through repeated peasant uprisings and growing anti-caste struggles.

The emergence of independent streams of Hindu, Muslim, Sikh politics in the late nineteenth and early twentieth centuries served to complicate matters further for the urban nationalists. Partition, and the establishment of the two independent nation states of India and Pakistan in 1947, led to calls on both sides of the border for full and unadulterated 'national-ness'. All this affected political positions and demands in India, as well as in Pakistan and, after the break-up of Pakistan in 1971, in Bangladesh. Thus, the question that has been repeatedly asked of Indian Muslims from 1947 to today: Are you an Indian first or a Muslim first?

It is a question that has been asked of other religious and ethnic minorities in India too – Christians, Eurasians or Anglo-Indians, at one point Sikhs, and in recent times also of Dalit (or ex-untouchable caste) activists, as they fight for jobs and opportunities for India's lowest castes. Significantly, the question is never asked of upper- and middle-caste, upper- and middle-class Hindus – or should I say, Hindu men – who are taken to be natural citizens, axiomatically Indian, undivided in their nationalism (even if they happen to be Shaivites and Vaishnavites, Brahman and Kshatriya, Lingayat and Vokkaliga, Patil and Choudhary).

It is hardly the case that anyone, anywhere chooses between the variety of different (caste, class, gender, religious and national) identities they inherit and inhabit. The demand for clear-cut choice becomes even more ridiculous in India in view of the nationalist claim that plurality and the celebration of plurality is precisely the sign of India's greatness. Yet, since the 1980s, and even more stridently today, the demand has been made that India's Muslims and Christians, and as I've noted at times even Sikhs, and various lower-caste and lower-class communities, must learn to live like 'Indians'. We must have one nation, one path, one uniform way of being. Difference is dangerous.

The fallout in the wake of the election of the current BJP government has been ominous. 'Hitherto, the discrimination and the distrust of the Muslim were covert,' writes a retired Muslim bureaucrat, presently a member of Parliament belonging to a small Opposition party: 'Now the gloves are off.' Thus, a BJP member of Parliament, Sakshi Maharaj, proclaims that 'madrasas [traditional Muslim schools] across the country are imparting the "education of terror" and "love jihad"' – the latter being a remarkable Hindu right-wing claim of a conspiracy of abduction, forced conversion and marriage of Hindu girls by trained and handsome Muslim boys – to increase the population of the Muslims.[3] And Sadhvi Niranjan Jyoti, another MP and minister in the BJP government, declared on the eve of the Delhi assembly elections of February 2015 that the choice was between '*Ram-zadas*' and '*haramzadas*' – to be admonished very gently by the prime minister (when Opposition parties demanded an apology and her resignation) with the exculpatory remark that she was after all just an ignorant villager.

This hostility to difference is in stark contrast to the widespread celebration of it by thinking Indians in the mid-twentieth century. Let me cite three rather different visions of Indianness, and its requirements, from that time. The first comes, unsurprisingly, from Mahatma Gandhi, staunch Hindu and unsurpassed national leader, whom even today's militant Hindu-nationalist government cannot disown. What would remain of the glory and uniqueness of Hinduism, Gandhi asked in one prayer meeting after another in the last months of his life before his assassination at the hands of a right-wing Hindu extremist in January 1948, if the Jama Masjid or Great Mosque in Delhi, where Muslims have gathered to worship ever since it was built by the Mughal Emperor Shah Jahan in the seventeenth century, no longer existed? What would Hindus become if they no longer believed what they have always believed, that divinity appears in an infinity of forms and places, and there are multiple paths to salvation?[4]

Another remarkable pronouncement appears in the 1966 Hindi novel, *Aadha Gaon*, by Rahi Masoom Raza, later the scriptwriter of the hugely popular TV serial version of the great Hindu epic, the Mahabharata: 'The Jan Sangh [the leading right-wing Hindu political party of the 1950s and 1960s, and predecessor of today's Bharatiya Janata Party] says the Muslims are outsiders. How can I say they're lying? But I must say that I belong to Ghazipur [a district in Uttar Pradesh, northern India]. My bonds with Gangauli [village] are unbreakable. It's not just a village, it's my home. Home. This word exists in every language and dialect. And that is why I repeat my statement – because Gangauli is not just a village, it's my home as well. "Because" – what a strong word this is. And there are thousands of "becauses" like it, and no sword is sharp enough to cut through the ties of this "because" ... And I give no one the right to say to me, "Rahi! You don't belong to Gangauli, and so get out and go, say, to Rae Bareli [a neighbouring district] ..."[5]

To that sense of home and belonging, I will add one last statement about the validity and value of the diverse inheritances each one of us lives with. It made for a particularly poignant moment in the Indian Constituent Assembly debate on the question of minority rights when Frank Anthony, the Anglo-Indian leader, referred to a comment sometimes made to him that he should drop the prefix 'Anglo' from his description of his community, if he was as strongly committed to India as he claimed. Anthony noted that, 'good or bad', 'right or wrong', the word Anglo-Indian 'connotes to me many things which I hold dear'. He went further: 'I will drop it readily, as soon as you drop your label ... The day you drop the label of "Hindu", the day you forget that you are a Hindu, that day – no, two days before that – I will drop by deed poll, by beat of drum if necessary, the prefix "Anglo".'[6] That day, the leader of the Anglo-Indians added, would be welcomed first and foremost by the minorities of India. For it would mean, of course, that there were no longer any minorities or majorities, at least in religious, racial or ethnic terms.

There is another side to 'minority' status and marginalization, however, which Frank Anthony could not address at that particular moment. This is a minority and margin produced by a parallel discourse, that of national development. In this discourse, the poor and the marginalized are presented as 'backward' and 'primitive', out-of-sync with the needs of the modern. They must be drawn into 'our' time – the time of development – however great the cost. Let me turn to this aspect of nationalism and democracy in contemporary India.

DEVELOPMENT AND ITS COSTS

It will help to begin, again, with another 'founding' document – in this instance the 'Draft National Policy for Rehabilitation of Persons

Displaced as a Consequence of Acquisition of Land', drawn up in 1994 in the wake of the Congress government's adoption of a 'New Economic Policy' embracing neo-liberal economics and globalization. The first few paragraphs of the draft policy deserve quotation at some length.[7]

1.1 With the advent of the New Economic Policy, it is expected that there will be large-scale investments, both on account of internal generation of capital and increased inflow of foreign investments, thereby creating an enhanced demand for land to be provided within a shorter time-span ...

1.2 Majority of our mineral resources, including coal, iron ore, and manganese reserves are located in the remote and backward regions mostly inhabited by tribals. Further, due to locational advantages of mineral-based resources, a strong industrial network has been created in these areas implying a cycle of positive growth.

1.3 The demand for land may exist in terms of thousands of acres of industrial and power mega-projects ... Likewise, there may be a demand for land for medium and small industrial projects, setting up of government offices, education and charitable institutions, which cumulatively add up to sizeable areas, though their immediate impact is not so perceptible ... Whatever might be the case, the process brings in its wake hardships to the persons whose lands contribute to the process of growth.

The last statement, about the dislocation and loss of livelihood suffered by significant numbers of people, is important. The population affected by the uprooting and displacement attendant on India's 'development' is reckoned by numerous commentators as being between thirty and fifty million in the forty years between 1951 and 1990 alone. Worldwide, in the 1980s and '90s, about ten million people annually entered the cycle of forced displacement and relocation in two sectors – dam construction and urban transportation – alone. At a conservative estimate, then, a World Bank official noted, about 90–100 million people had been uprooted during the decade 1985–95. These were, he emphasized, partial figures, not including people forced out by the development of forests and reserve parks, mining and thermal power plant construction, and numerous other development projects.[8]

The Government of India's 1994 Draft National Policy for Rehabilitation accepted that at least 16.5 million persons had been 'displaced by various categories of projects' in the years up to 1985, and that 75 per cent of them were 'still awaiting rehabilitation' – forty years after the beginning of planned development. Tribal peasants, who made up just under 8 per cent of India's total population, accounted for 40 per cent of the displaced persons. Roughly one-tenth of India's indigenous peoples – as they would be called in other parts of the world – had thus become refugees in their own land. More evictions had followed with the adoption of the New Economic Policy and the increasing pace of development in the 1990s.

These are, in the words of the Draft National Policy, the 'hardships' that some 'persons' inevitably suffer in furthering the goals of development. The 'National Rehabilitation and Resettlement Policy', elaborated by the Government of India's Ministry of Rural Development in 2007, puts it more bluntly: 'Provision of public facilities or infrastructure often requires the exercise of legal powers by the state under the principle of *eminent domain* for acquisition of private property, leading to involuntary displacement of people, depriving them of their land, livelihood and shelter; restricting their access to traditional resource base, and uprooting them from their socio-cultural environment. These have traumatic, psychological and socio-cultural consequences on the affected population which call for protecting their rights, in particular of the weaker sections of the society including members of the Scheduled Castes, Scheduled Tribes, marginal farmers and women.'[9]

The colonial-era language of 'eminent domain' comes from an earlier founding, colonial-era document – the Land Acquisition Act of 1894, which was amended marginally in 1984. The discourse of development and its inevitable costs stems from the independent government's concern to modernize and catch up with the West. Notice the unquestioned theme in the 'sympathetic' statements of national policy on rehabilitation and compensation cited above: growth, large-scale investment, mega projects, positive growth. If national integration was a primary concern at the time of Partition and Independence of the Indian subcontinent, and national integrity, internal security, public safety, etc., have remained critical ever since, there is another overriding concern in the articulation of the 'national interest' now. It is captured in the refrain, modernization, development, economic growth – goals that necessitate the resuscitation of colonial-era laws and land acquisition for 'public purposes'. The most recent steps in this direction take the form of an ordinance propounded in the last days of 2014 to make the acquisition of land easier, and even less amenable to the objection of the public at large or for that matter, the affected landowners.

This Ordinance Raj is only another step in the disempowerment of landowners – rich and, more frequently, poor. The Government of India, and elite opinion in general, has no doubt about the necessity and ineluctability of 'the costs of national development', and there is little discussion about who is to bear them. Paragraph 1.2 of the 2007 National Rehabilitation and Resettlement Policy statement puts the point succinctly: 'There is imperative need to recognize rehabilitation and resettlement issues as *intrinsic to the development process*' (emphasis added).

The matter of compensation for land acquired for 'national development' is compounded by the fact that the poor among the displaced frequently have no written title to the land, even when they've lived and worked on it for generations. Just as often, there is no cultivable land available to compensate their losses. To say nothing of the lack of political will on the part of local-level leaders and bureaucrats to provide such compensation. The investigative journalist, P. Sainath, documents the results in his remarkable 1996 book, *Everybody Loves a Good Drought*. The provocation in the title is deliberate: for, as the author notes, drought, like development, has become a profitable industry for numbers of intermediaries and lower-level functionaries charged with implementing government policy.[10]

Sainath cites numerous cases in which extremely poor people across the country have been removed from their homes to make way for 'firing ranges, jet fighter plants, coal mines, power projects, dams, sanctuaries, prawn and shrimp farms, even poultry farms'. These are the people, he notes, who pay the 'price' of development for the rich who run the nation. One of his examples – from the village of Chikapar in Koraput district in the state of Odisha – powerfully illustrates the point.

In 1968, the land of the village was acquired for a Hindustan Aeronautics Limited project to manufacture engines for MiG jet fighters. 'We didn't know where to go,' Mukta Kadam, a tribal peasant woman, told Sainath. 'We just went because the *saab log* [the sahibs, bureaucrats or bosses] told us to go.' Evicted at short notice, the villagers resettled on other land they owned – which they named 'Chikapar' again. Many received no compensation for their displacement. In 1987, Chikapar residents were evicted once more from this second location, which the author calls 'Chikapar-2'. With considerable effort, the villagers established a third Chikapar. This time they were spread out in several little pockets, still largely on their own lands. In the early 1990s, they were served with eviction notices for a third time. The revenue inspector of the area confirmed that a third round of notices had been served: 'They are encroachers and must go.' 'Encroachers,' let us note, on their own land. 'Chikapar,' Sainath noted, 'is being chased by development.'[11]

The rush to expand India's coal mining industry will serve as a final illustration of current thinking on 'progress'. As a relatively poor country, set on joining the company of developed nations, India must and will get its power where it can, the country's present power minister Piyush Goyal has declared. The repercussions – consequences for climate change, or effects on the native population – are simply 'regrettable': part of the cost of growth. A visiting journalist describes the city of Dhanbad, a major town in a coal mining region in the state of Jharkhand, as resembling 'a post-apocalyptic movie set, with villages surrounded by barren slag heaps half-obscured by acrid smoke spewing from a century-old fire slowly burning through the buried coal seams'. Social activists allege that coal companies and bureaucrats have allowed such fires to burn and spread poisonous fumes in order to drive the local population away. T.K. Lahiry, chairman of a government-owned company in the area, Bharat Coking Coal Limited, denies that the government deliberately neglects the fires and the fumes, but agrees that tens of thousands of local inhabitants 'must be displaced' for 'India' to realize its coal energy needs. 'Evictions are done too slowly,' he says.[12] Hence the new ordinance to ease the process of land acquisition for mines, without even the fig leaf of a bill introduced in Parliament before the government resorts to the ordinance.

The discourse of development and growth outlined above puts a rather sobering light on the rousing speech delivered by Narendra Modi before an exultant crowd of thousands of people of Indian origin who had gathered at Madison Square Garden, New York, on 28 September 2014. Let us consider the speech in concluding this reflection on development, democracy and difference: 'India is the biggest democracy in the world ... We have three powers that nobody else has, and it is our duty to identify these powers, present them to the world and mobilize them: *Democracy* this is our biggest strength. Even the poorest man went out in the heat to hear speeches; *Demographic dividend* – 65 per cent of people less than the age of thirty-five years; *Demand* [given our population of 2.5 billion] ... We want to make development a mass movement ... I invite you to come "*Make in India*". If you want human resources and low-cost production, India is your destination.'

Come and 'Make in India,' Modi urges the gathering of rich, nostalgic 'non-resident Indians', living in America and imagining the India of their dreams – a dream in which the poor have largely disappeared. All that India's leader has to say about the poor in this speech to the rich is that many of the poorest citizens came out to hear election speeches in the extreme heat of April and May 2014. He does not say anything about the role of money and the propaganda blitz in bringing them out. To the well-to-do, and especially the well-to-do living in the advanced, capitalist West who happen to hail from India, the prime minister extends an open invitation. They should come back – in spirit, and in wealth, if not in person – to the largest democracy in the world, where capital investment is sorely needed and labour is cheap. India will welcome them with a red carpet, not red tape, as he has proclaimed in many statements. The country will clean up its offices and hotels, the tourist sites along the rivers, and the access roads from the airports. It will do all it can to keep the poor out of sight.

It is part of the same endeavour that leads the BJP government to pull back on the funding of schemes like the Mahatma Gandhi National Rural Employment Guarantee Act (MGNREGA), a law by which one member of every poor rural household in the country was guaranteed employment for at least 100 days in the year, at the minimum wage, which averaged Rs 132 (just over $2 in 2014) per day. Policymakers may be proud of the fact that India was the first country in the world to have created such a scheme, and may recognize too that it helped thousands, or hundreds of thousands, of poor families in the countryside, especially among tribal peasants and the lowest castes, to survive somehow. The

Government of India knows too that it can withdraw the scheme only at its own peril. Nevertheless, it has decided in the 2014–15 budget to do no more than renew overall funding at the reduced levels of 2012–13 and 2013–14, when the costs and the needs of the scheme are clearly greater.[13]

A FINAL WORD

The welfare and togetherness of all – *sabka saath, sabka vikas* – remains the declared goal of India's political leaders. However, as the above paragraphs should have made clear, it plays itself out in dangerous ways today. Those who are not devotees, or rather self-declared followers of the Hindu god Rama, are pronounced traitors ('haramzadas'). Poor Muslims and Christians are subjected to 'ghar wapsi' ('return to the fold') Hindu conversion programmes. Alongside, we have the emergence of a remarkably segregated society, in religious as well as class terms. In the nation's capital region, the super-rich increasingly live in gated communities, Lutyens's Delhi has been taken over largely by the politically powerful and well connected, while the majority of the population lives in slums and hovels hidden behind the multistoreyed buildings and overcrowded flyovers of the developing mega city.

We can almost hear the whisper: The country cannot afford anything different; the poor and the 'minorities' must join the mainstream and fend for themselves – as the rich so obviously do.

NOTES

1   By a subsequent constitutional amendment, passed in 1978, the Republic of India was declared to be 'socialist' and 'secular' in addition to sovereign and democratic.

2   The quotations from Gandhi, Malaviya and Lajpat Rai in this and succeeding paragraphs are taken from Gyanendra Pandey, *The Construction of Communalism in Colonial North India* (New Delhi, Oxford India Perennials, 2012), 211, 236 and 259.

3   Abdul Khaliq, 'Like Never Before, I the Muslim am seen as the root cause of nation's problems', *Indian Express,* 27 September 2014.

4   See Gyanendra Pandey, *Routine Violence. Nations, Fragments, Histories* (Stanford: Stanford University Press, 2006), 158.

5   Rahi Masoom Raza, *Aadha Gaon* (New Delhi: Rajkamal Prakashan, 1966), 303–305. See also the translation of the novel by Gillian Wright, *The Feuding Families of Gangauli* (New Delhi: Penguin Books, 1995), 290–291.

6   *Constituent Assembly Debates, Official Report,* Vol. VIII (16 May to 16 June 1949), 329.

7   Government of India, Ministry of Rural Development, 'Draft National Policy for Rehabilitation of Persons Displaced as a Consequence of Acquisition of Land', undated. The draft seems to have been circulated in several versions with minor variations, with some being marked 'secret'. I cite the draft as published in *Economic and Political Weekly,* 15 June 1996.

8   For figures cited in this and the next paragraph, see Jai Sen, 'National Rehabilitation Policy. A Critique', *Economic and Political Weekly* (hereafter, *EPW*), 4 February 1995; Chittaroopa Palit, 'Short-changing the Displaced. National Rehabilitation Policy', *EPW,* 3 July 2004; Abhijit Guha, 'Resettlement and Rehabilitation. First National Policy', *EPW,* 12 November 2005; Michael M. Cernea, 'Understanding and Preventing Impoverishment from Displacement: Reflections on the State of Knowledge', *Journal of Refugee Studies,* Vol. 8, No. 3 (1995); and P. Sainath, *Everybody Loves a Good Drought. Stories from India's Poorest Districts* (New Delhi: Penguin Books, 1996), 71–75.

9   Government of India, Ministry of Rural Development, 'The National Rehabilitation and Resettlement Policy, 2007', published in the Gazette of India, Extraordinary, Part I, Section I, 31 October 2007, para. 1.1 (emphasis in original). The Scheduled Castes and Scheduled Tribes refer to ex-untouchable and tribal peasant groups, socially stigmatized and economically amongst the most depressed sections

of India's population, who were listed in special 'schedules' drawn up and appended to the Indian Constitution adopted in 1950.

10 Sainath, *Everybody Loves a Good Drought,* 320, 362.

11 Ibid., 88–93.

12 Gardiner Harris, 'Coal Rush in India Could Tip Balance on Climate Change,' *New York Times*, 18 November 2014.

13 Brinda Karat, 'Ending Destitution and Distress', *The Hindu*, 25 October 2014.

Conservatism and the Cult of the Individual in a Populist Age

Shruti Kapila

꧁

Shruti Kapila lectures and researches on modern Indian history, political thought and global history at the Faculty of History, and is fellow and director of studies at Corpus Christi College, University of Cambridge. She is editor of *An Intellectual History for India* (CUP, 2010) and co-editor of *Political Thought in Action: The Bhagavad Gita and Modern India* (CUP, 2013).

Having initially bucked the fate of liberal democracies elsewhere in the world, India has belatedly gone 'conservative'. In recent decades, Western democracies have witnessed the erosion of voter participation but the consolidation of conservative politics. The Modi mandate has declared a new form of 'conservatism' – a political language that has ushered in the 'individual' as the totem of change to direct India's future. Little wonder then that Modi himself is compared to strong figures from recent and contemporary world history, from Hitler to Thatcher and Putin to Erdogan, united as they are by their arch determinism to direct the course of history. But like much else, things in India look like things elsewhere, but crucially, are never quite the same.

Conservatism, the arch creed which preserves and conserves, has a long history going back to the origins of parliamentary democracy during the classic age of revolutions. Back in its hoary tradition, its figurehead Edmund Burke looked at raging revolutions straight in the eye, just when 'people' in France and America killed off kings and dethroned an empire with sheer collective will. To be sure, the main conservative idea then was to be 'cool' in the heat of change so as to preserve old privilege. And so it did. Britain remains a monarchy. In India today, conservatism has acquired a kind of revolutionary import, in that it is the byword for change. Overwhelmingly, the Modi mandate is certainly not about protecting old privilege. Quite the opposite. It is all about validating the new.

Benares, the perpetually old city of India, or Varanasi as it is called today that is Modi's constituency, has a habit of concealing the new. On the face of it, the city represents heightened Hindu piety that is on daily display at its iconic ghats. As the symbolic capital of Hinduism, it is no surprise that Modi, the leader of Hindu nationalism, chose to represent it. This is also where upper-caste Hindus prefer to go and die. Yet, in its modern incarnation, Varanasi has been the city of arrival of the new. It was the city that birthed commercial capital in India.

On the eve of the British Empire in India while Europe was in revolutionary mode, a new commercial force of bankers, magnates, creditors and traders poured their money into temples and ghats that appear today as the timeless architecture of Varanasi. Predominantly Hindu and urban, this new social group helped pull the rug under the formidable Mughal Empire with their sheer commercial power that controlled trading and credit networks pulling India into emerging global capitalist horizons. Varanasi became the defining midpoint to the dominating and belligerent Englishman's Calcutta – now Kolkata and the fast fading Mughal Empire's seat in Delhi. Whether they were Marwaris or banias, they traded with the expansionist East India Company, and provided credit to warring Indian rulers. We know how that story ended. The British violently closed the gap that had appeared between a new Indian commercial prowess and an old political power, and dominated the subcontinent for nearly two centuries. The British Empire is mercifully long gone.

The 2014 general election, dubbed as the 'economy election' with Varanasi as its epicentre, has also closed the wedge that has reappeared between the new economic order and political power. Big, but relatively young, business houses such as the Ambani and Adani groups gained a billion-plus dollars in value overnight as soon as the results became official. With unprecedented influence on the political process, and in part through the media, new money and entrepreneurial activity has set abuzz the political landscape with aspiration. Few tell us what aspiration stands for. The new, first-time and young voter armed with a collective number of 100 million, has overwhelmingly turned its back on India's independent history and has aspired for change. They – and other not so young Indians – have helped close the gap between money and power, and from below as it were, casting their lot with India Inc. and its political figurehead of Modi. The assumption and aspiration is that the wealthy will generate a form of growth that will be experienced by individuals, even those who are far removed from Dalal Street. It is a plea and a mandate for capitalism from bottom up, if there was ever one.

If you are a Marxist reading this, this is the point where you shout 'false consciousness'. Which is to say that they who have voted thus just don't know what they have done, indeed they have voted against their own self-interest! This is the quintessential conundrum that has allowed conservatism to become the pre-eminent force of democracy in the world. Workers and the labouring poor mandated the regimes of Margaret Thatcher, Ronald Reagan and George W. Bush. The entrenched powers of the trade unions and the state were broken and diluted in favour of enterprising self-help with a faith in the magic of markets even as inequality grew in direct proportion to wealth. For Anglo-America, it was not about the new versus the old, but about turning Right.

HISTORICAL REVERSAL

'Conservative' India, however, has appeared on a curious historical reversal of the old and the new. The Congress, the party that stood for national change and development, was judged by the latest mandate as the old guard with a stench of stasis hanging over it. It was targeted as the obstacle to change. The hundred-odd-year robust Indian left and liberal tradition that was later institutionalized in the Nehruvian state is being dismantled by the Modi mandate.

New and conservative India is the opposite and mirror image of national India that Jawaharlal Nehru discovered, invented and owned. In the old nationalist days, conservatism in India was much like what Burke wanted it to be. With an impulse to preserve, a form of 'Hindu populism' was also birthed in Varanasi, a century ago. Stalwarts like Madan Mohan Malaviya restrained Nehru's dependence on the English language in favour of Hindi, and his desire for a religion-free political vocabulary. Other Hindu populists like P.D. Tandon weighed on Nehru, thus stalling the reform of the Hindu Code Bill and in the process killing B.R. Ambedkar's career and radical plans in the first decade of free India. Most famously, at the moment of Independence, Sardar Patel invited the then hub of conservatism, namely, the Hindu Mahasabha, to join the Congress. The power of the Left–liberal tradition was such that it could incorporate a weak conservatism within its big-tent approach to politics. Even the southern stalwart

(C. Rajagopalachari) Rajaji's attempt to have a separate conservative party led to the stillborn Swatantra Party. At that point only the communists ducked the Congress zeal for incorporation as a means to dilute political competition, but in the process became a social democratic rather than a revolutionary force.

Yet, the single continual thread of conservatism that has existed since the onset of mass politics in India, and through the Nehru era, is its avowed and consistent commitment to free market even as it changed party forms from the Mahasabha, to the Jana Sangh and now the Bharatiya Janata Party (BJP). Hinduism provides the spiritual succour, as much as identity, to the hard knocks that brutal and anonymous market participation entails.

The conservatives are the new radicals of India. Varanasi once again, as in previous centuries, captures and symbolizes change. Anti-history, and to that extent revolutionary, this mandate is directed towards the future. What that will be would be to witness history. Nevertheless, the market today has acquired a new and powerful political presence.

Equally, this 'conservative' revolution has assumed to reinterpret and change the national script. If, for Nehru, the state was the agent of delivering the national project, for today's conservatism, 'New India', as it is increasingly referred to, has a zealous faith in the cult of the individual. At the centre of this mandate has been the figure of Modi who seeks to represent this idea of New India and the marshalling, on the face of it, of what can be termed an identity-free identity. The individual magnified in the form of the leader and its followers are increasingly recast as 'free' individuals ready for market participation and ostensibly detached from their social inheritances.

STRONGMAN OR THE LEADER'S PARTY

The biggest and what felt like the longest election season on the planet ended on 14 May 2014 in India. Narendra Modi's victory bucked at least one trend: since the start of the millennium, financial markets, the media and the opinion polls had called the elections wrong. But Modi started off and remained the favourite of bookies, the press and pundits. Even before he was installed as the centre of Delhi's forbidding architecture of power, Modi and his campaign had changed the political landscape, heralding the arrival of a presidential style of politics in the world's largest parliamentary democracy: a phenomenon which will have consequences. The electoral campaign, above all, seemed as though one man had asked more than 800 million eligible voters to take part in a plebiscite on his personality and politics.

With record levels of voter participation – in some states over 80 per cent with the national average in the high sixties – Modi dominated the election narrative. Anecdotal evidence and press commentary suggest that Indians craved a strong leader. It is in this context that he was, and is, compared to other strong world figures, mostly to Thatcher and Hitler. Others argue that Modi has much in common with Russia's Vladimir Putin, a comparison that goes well beyond a shared pride in their manly chest sizes.

The instructive comparison, though, comes from India's own democratic history. Indira Gandhi destroyed the internal structures of her own party, which had not taken her leadership candidature seriously, and emerged in the early 1970s as the first person after independence to be completely identified with India. She cast herself in opposition to a sinister 'foreign hand', which became an excuse for remodelling India's politics and its institutions. In government, the executive arrogated powers for itself that have endured ever since. Party bosses and big men, or the 'Congress system', as it was quaintly called (these were people who had converted an anti-colonial movement into a monopolistic powerhouse) were all suborned to take part in the cult and charisma of Mrs Gandhi. With a heady dose of populism and authoritarianism, she ensured that the party, the nation – even dissent itself – were all identified with her. Slogans such as 'Indira is India' were only matched by the urgent, if unheeded, calls to 'end poverty'. The twin themes of economic development and political violence were as dominant then as they are now. In overwhelming a tired and fragmented Congress, she redirected and controlled its political fortunes, and India was transformed in the process.

MODI AND THE RSS

Much like Indira Gandhi, Modi has had to contend with party bigwigs and marginalize those who had made the BJP into an electoral force in the past. If the so-called Modi wave swept all before it, rivals within the party were among the victims of the sweeping. But, unlike the Congress, powerful bodies affiliated to the BJP will pose a significant challenge to Modi's one-man political machine. Strikingly, it is the transformation and resurgence of one such affiliate – said to be the largest volunteer body in the world – that has helped secure Modi's power base. With a reputation for violence and a historic aversion to direct political power, the Rashtriya Swayamsevak Sangh (RSS) and its proximity to Modi have burdened him with a Faustian bargain.

Congress regimes of the twentieth century sought to manage the use of violence with limited success. Having lost its political monopoly in the 1970s and '80s, and on the eve of an era of coalition politics in India, Congress governments presided over riots and insurgencies across the country. It all seemed to bear out the political thinker Hannah Arendt's assertion that weak regimes indulge in violence. One might add that weak regimes coupled with strong leaders have made for a deadly combination. The erstwhile stalwarts of Indian journalism such as Arun Shourie and M.J. Akbar assiduously recorded these tactics and held Mrs Gandhi's government to account in print for its record of riots. Today, both men are with the BJP.

One of the unsung achievements of the decade of Congress rule, headed by a famously weak leader in the form of Prime Minister

Manmohan Singh, was a relatively riot-free India. As is well known, Modi, the strong man from Gujarat, has a dubious record on riots and violence. The BJP's initial capture of political power in the early 1990s, with L.K. Advani's juggernaut for the Ram temple, was marked by an unprecedented mobilization of violence. On the eve of the May 2014 elections, if the violence that broke out in Assam is taken seriously, arguably, violence has a habit of preceding the BJP's ascendance to electoral power. For the Congress in the old days, by contrast, it was the fear of losing power that produced the context and cause of violence. What is not in doubt is that media allure has started to command a premium in India's increasingly modern election campaigns that favour the magnetic charms of an individual in the Modi mould over and above grim issues and the sheer grit of political ideas.

Having become prime minister, the question for Modi is whether he will be allowed to behave like an executive president in a parliamentary system. With its reliance on a single, charismatic leader, the BJP looks a lot like Congress under Indira Gandhi. Modi is confident, but it is his party that could face an identity crisis. After all, it was the claims of identity politics that had made the BJP into an electoral force when it first assumed power towards the end of the last century.

IDENTITY-FREE INDIA?

Identity, as we know, became the big idea of Indian democracy twenty years ago. 'Mandal' (a reference to B.P. Mandal Commission's report on caste reservations), 'Mandir' (Ram Temple–Babri Masjid dispute) and 'Market' (media shorthand for caste, religion and a new economic order) made identity the mantra of what was dubbed India's 'second democratic upsurge'. Today, it is the individual who dominates as the big idea with Modi, Media and Market appearing triumphant. The cult of 'Moditva' has replaced Hindutva as the rallying call of aspiration, in which an individual can loom over a party and set out to direct, if not change, history. This is precisely why individual figures from India's founding moment – from Gandhi to Patel – are being restaged to announce that a 'great man' can change the context. What is at stake, though, is the legacy of Nehru and Ambedkar who installed the state and society as the logic of Indian democracy.

The individual, at first sight, seems to have replaced the identity politics of the 1990s. The market, combined with an unprecedented urban expansion, has together propelled the individual and his appeals to history at the centre of the new political discourse. Not since the slogan of 'Indira is India' has one individual directed political attention in the way Modi has done. The end of Indira's India opened a new sequence of politics in which society in the form of caste gained political control. In the 1990s, caste blocked the ascendant politics of religion.

Today, Modi signifies the archetypical individual. An OBC (backward class) leading a pre-eminent party of identity, caste and Hindutva remain conspicuously absent in his rhetoric. However, it would be erroneous to suggest that this duel is over. Chillingly, the Muzaffarnagar riots in August–September 2013 and, less ominously, Jat assertions for legal recognition as OBC in Rajasthan and Punjab demonstrate otherwise. The BJP's sudden squeamishness towards its own campaign for building a Ram Mandir on the spot where Babri Masjid (demolished by BJP/RSS activists in December 1992) once stood shows that though Hindutva is the base of its politics yet it does not want to speak in its name.

The 'aam aadmi' (common man), by contrast, has become the counter-cult figure to Modi. Like Modi, the aam aadmi is seen to be stripped of his social inheritance, be it caste or religion. The idea of the 'aam' seeks to project ordinariness as common cause and identity. In a country marked by distinctions, a populist victimhood by precisely those in urban and semi-urban India, who have made relative gains by market reforms, identifies the aam aadmi. The Aam Aadmi Party's (AAP) individual is painstakingly portrayed as a modest sufferer.

Modi and the aam aadmi signal the immediacy of the present in which the individual, however big or ordinary, is projected to overcome history. Saviour or sufferer, the projected powers of the individual thus are aspirational, extraordinary and even potent enough to change history. Such a discourse is an outcome of the 'mediatization' of politics and in sync with the market. History, as opposed to society, is being selectively mobilized as evidence of the individual's power.

The stupefying power of the media has reduced history to a game of symbolic thrones. Mimicking Gandhi's hard-won political strategies, AAP responded and reduced the power of Gandhian symbols to fight a powerful system to a reality TV show. Modi too has laid claim to the nation's founders from Patel to Gandhi; even Lal Bahadur Shastri hasn't escaped his assiduous poaching.

The Congress has history on its side but appears immobilized by its burden. Its commitment to the invisible, non-individual, but still overwhelmingly rural base of India has resulted in neither a slogan nor vision. Focused on the social, it is struggling to create a new narrative for the future. Modi's campaign has dismissed its welfare strategies as mere handouts, suggesting instead that the state should enable the market.

BANISHING NEHRU, AMBEDKAR

By attaching himself to the founding pantheon, Modi is claiming the future. When he talks of a popular movement for development, the missing founding figure is Nehru, who established the political language of development in India. Yet, ironically, in an election speech entirely indebted to Nehru's vocabulary, Modi sought to disconnect ideas of development away from Nehru and the state.

In championing his own rise as a member of the OBC but without the help of state reservations, Modi would have wished to expel and banish another founding figure, namely B.R. Ambedkar. Ambedkar is synonymous with the Indian democratic project, and his ideas tied

India's destiny not to the individual projected by Modi, but to society. In appropriating Patel, Modi wants to signal the strength of individual action over ideas that defined the Sardar in relation to the national pantheon and his political peers. If Nehru advocated state development, Ambedkar enshrined the logic of social justice in the political realm.

A word here about Ambedkar's often misunderstood advocacy of caste-based reservations. When he laid the foundations of the democratic architecture of India, reservations were seen as a non-violent solution to historic inequality. Reservations were not only about jobs or education. Rather, Ambedkar transformed the potential social strife of caste and its inherent antagonism into open, democratic and political competition. Above all, it meant that the political would subsume rather than transcend the social. To detach the social from the political, in the name of an ostensibly identity-free individual now, is not only to misrecognize Indian democracy but, more dangerously, to evacuate politics of its content.

Though focused on the issue of caste, Ambedkar pointed to the then prevalent impoverished understanding of wider political issues. For, as he argued, sovereignty, especially in democracies, lies not with the individual sovereign but resides within the social. Even a cursory glance at India's democratic history attests to the new social majorities whether they are moored in region or caste. Heterogeneous and reactive by nature, social majorities nevertheless ensure the contingency of the political.

Far from having disappeared, the social in India's democratic history has appeared in various forms, and at each juncture has redefined the political matrix. In the 1950s and '60s, the Congress consensus was challenged by parties seeking recognition of linguistic identities. The communist parties, on the other hand, asserted with a degree of success the nature of 'class' configurations. The 1970s and '80s, however, witnessed the domination of regional parties which demanded federalism through a diverse play of region, language and caste, even religion as in the case of Punjab and militant Sikhism. In each instance, the dominant and national party, namely the Congress, got redefined inasmuch as its political fortunes waxed and waned in the face of these contestations.

Today, in less than nine months of Modi's majority mandate, the newly formed party of the common man or the Aam Aadmi Party has put a stop to Modi's sweep and complete domination of the electoral landscape by resoundingly and completely overwhelming the Delhi assembly elections held in February 2015. While it might be too early to forecast whether this is the new source of opposition on a national scale, it is nevertheless possible to say that this is evidence of the social to articulate new constellations. In this instance, the individual cult of the aam aadmi has tapped into the wider discourse of aspiration, but this time in the name of modesty rather than in the vein of an assertive muscularity of the individual parading Hindu nationalism. In short, it has positioned a populist and modest counter-individual as a political stakeholder to the strident Hindu nationalist. This has, at the very least, shown that the political cannot overwhelm the social entirely.

AAP OR OPPOSITION OF THE ORDINARY

There is nothing aam or ordinary about the aam aadmi or the ordinary man. The capture of the capital city points only to the extraordinary arrival of a party in its name on the Indian democratic landscape. Though specific to Indian conditions, the arrival of such a politics is not unique in the contemporary moment. Across the global south, from Tahrir to Taksim Square, the opening years of this decade have seen the so-called ordinary person bursting into visible prominence. Although appearances of global commonality might be deceptive, it is significant that Delhi's sprawling, if fortressed, architecture of political power, has of late witnessed similar congregations of the claimed common or the aam aadmi.

AAP has created a political rhetoric that focuses on the urgency of the present, a demand of the 'here and now'. A brief historical genealogy is instructive. In a rhetoric filled with 'anti-this and anti-that', it was anti-Congressism in the first instance that gave AAP its raison d'être. At the height of the Indian nation's love affair with Nehru, Ram Manohar Lohia had famously coined 'anti-Congressism', signalling exhaustion with a single national party and anger at dynastic power. In the 1960s, this politics of negation powerfully unseated Congress hegemony in several states. In a decade not entirely dissimilar to the current one, then as now, both violent and non-violent communist and radical movements had appeared in the countryside. While agrarian capitalism and inadequate land reforms were significant issues then, today, even as those older problems continue to persist, land has become the single largest issue, in town and country alike.

Anti-Congress, anti-English and anti-upper-caste, Lohia's project was not a mere sum of negations. A distinctive, if now forgotten, brand of socialism that had as much Gandhi as it had Marx, made Lohia not only an astute politician who changed the given equation of numbers, but also a major political thinker, if not a visionary. A synthetic thinker, Lohia navigated but departed from established political languages of the day and repeatedly returned to the social question. From public expenditure to entitlement and from considerations on violence to foreign policy, Lohia mobilized the pen, the courtroom and the very object of democracy, 'people'.

The ironic legacy of Lohia is that he is seen to be, and with some justification, the thinker behind the political and legal empowerment of the Other Backward Castes. The 'social' or the 'people' were increasingly identified in this project and by some of his successors as the OBC. Though Lohia coined and occasionally used the term aam aadmi, it did not gain any attention then. Was it an untimely term? Or is it that the aam aadmi belongs not so much to the social logic but to the pall of populism?

In the intervening decades, Lohia's inventive logic of coalitions became ascendant with the OBC emerging as a major, if not the greatest, beneficiary of such a political mathematics. Mobilizations too multiplied as they became complex and 'mediatized'. Advani's rath yatra that captured television screens followed the legal empowerment of the OBC in the 1990s, and inaugurated a democratic, if contested, mandate for Hindtuva. Like AAP today, there were others who made spectacular entries, whether it was N.T. Rama Rao, or more recently Mamata Bannerjee who appealed, above all, to a populist sentiment. It is an empowered populism today that has propelled another kind of individual in its small, modest incarnation to the dominant figure of Modi.

POLITICAL POPULISM

Bursting between the bipartisan poles of the Delhi city state, the Aam Aadmi Party (AAP) has articulated anger and exhaustion. It is a curious underdog which has, unsurprisingly, received a rapturous response from a powerful media. Shorn initially of a political project, AAP has instead created equivalence between different demands and issues. Corruption, dynastic power, household bills, amenities, rape and sexuality, all appear alike, demanding attention and inciting rage. Inherent to its populist logic, sentiment and a sanctimonious disposition is key to AAP's political performance. This equivalence is, however, marked by a common antagonist or enemy, namely established political power and arguably, parliamentary democracy itself.

A few critics have argued that devoid of politics, AAP is a sign of our neo-liberal times where efficiency and transparency trump more traditional political concerns, not least equality and social justice. Not entirely untrue, the current urban thrust of the party has, nevertheless, cut across sections and looks increasingly like a popular unity rather than a class unity. The logic of the social that, in the

Indian case, unmistakably carries the signature of caste is singularly, if not ominously, absent. In an age of ascendant Hindutva and a time of resurgent riots, only the deliberately ignorant can declare this phenomenon as the end of identity politics.

A mere taunt from an established Congressman converted this 'movement' into a significant player in party politics. Though now not elusive, political power is likely to trigger an identity crisis for the celebrated arriviste. Now the question of responsibility for its mandate will force the party to confront its antagonism to political power and establishment. If the 'people' of democracy are neither a caste nor class but only signifies an ordinary anger of extraordinary proportions and heightened perceptions of disempowerment, AAP looks less like its urban global counterparts.

Instead, AAP can be compared to another configuration, but from America. American democracy, which AAP leader Arvind Kejriwal cited approvingly, has seen the populist appeal of the Tea Party that also authentically speaks to the concerns of the so-called ordinary and the seemingly disempowered in a bipartisan establishment. The Tea Party too mobilized an important symbol from America's anti-colonial struggle much like the Gandhi Nehru cap that now announces the aam aadmi.

AAP's achievement thus is not the wedge in bipartisan poles that have appeared with regularity, inasmuch as India's political landscape remains intransigent to the bipartisanism of the Anglo-American variety. Rather, the aam aadmi's main achievement is its name, which as of now remains a name without content. Now with the formation of an AAP government in the city state of Delhi, it could be challenged by its own aversion to established power; and with each electoral success it will be suborned to strictures and norms that define routine party politics. Established political power can potentially take its anti-establishment edge away. In a similar way, the strident and violent identity politics of Hindutva has already begun to chip away at the shine of ostensibly identity-free Modi mandate. Conservatism and its nemesis, populism, archly represented by Modi and Kejriwal as icons, have propelled the cult of the individual and its hitherto unforeseen consequences to the centre of Indian politics. Both favour the individual. Transcending, let alone trouncing, the social will prove chimerical. The protean yet powerful force of the social, that currently remains unclaimed, nevertheless points to the potential and political trajectory of Indian democracy.

The Question of Fascism

Radhika Desai

~ɤ~

Radhika Desai is professor at the Department of Political Studies, University of Manitoba, Winnipeg, Canada, and director of the Geopolitical Economy Research Group there. She is the author of *Geopolitical Economy: After US Hegemony, Globalization and Empire* (2013), *Slouching Towards Ayodhya: From Congress to Hindutva in Indian Politics* (2004), and *Intellectuals and Socialism: 'Social Democrats' and the Labour Party* (1994), co-editor of *Revitalizing Marxist Theory for Today's Capitalism* (2010) and editor of *Theoretical Engagements in Geopolitical Economy* (2015) and *Developmental and Cultural Nationalisms* (2009).

The question of Hindutva's fascist character is an old one, having exercised leaders of the Congress party well before Independence. It came up again in the 1970s when Indira Gandhi flung accusations of fascism at the Rashtriya Swayamsevak Sangh (RSS) as it put its organized muscle into the JP movement (led by Gandhian socialist leader Jayaprakash Narayan) against her rule.

The Youth Congress, headed by Sanjay Gandhi, which mobilized lumpen youth (and even deployed the imagery of the monkey god, Hanuman, anticipating the imagery of the Sangh Parivar's own Bajrang Dal, in his car factory, if not more widely) gave Mrs Gandhi's Emergency a semblance of fascism. However, few today think of the Congress in these terms.

After the Sangh Parivar organized the macabre destruction of Babri mosque in 1992, the question of Hindutva's fascism took on a more menacing significance. The clearly staged spectacle suggested so many parallels with fascism that they could hardly be ignored.[1] Aijaz Ahmad enumerated a great many such parallels succinctly:

> What I am suggesting is that in its staging of spectacles, in its techniques of mobilisations, in the multiplicity of its fronts, in the shadowy traffic between its parliamentary and non-parliamentary organs, in the seamless interplay of form and content in its ideological interpellations, in the connection it asserts between a resurgent national tradition and the regaining of masculinist virility, in its simultaneous claims to legality and extra-legality, in its construction of a mythic history which authorises it to be above history, and in its organization of a *dharm sansad* that authorises it to be above the civil parliament whenever it so chooses, the Sangh Parivar is a classically fascist force with large Indian twists of course, as every fascism must always take a specifically national form.[2]

The Sangh Parivar and its member organizations, the Bharatiya Janata Party (BJP), the Vishwa Hindu Parishad (VHP), the Bajrang Dal and the parent organization, the RSS (or simply Sangh), organized the demolition of Babri mosque as a culmination of a series of mobilizations in the late 1980s and early 1990s. They were designed to bring the BJP out of the electoral abyss of a mere two seats in the Lok Sabha into which the 1984 general elections had cast it.

Considering that the first attempt on the mosque was made in 1990, as recorded in Anand Patwardhan's enduring 1992 documentary, *Raam Ke Naam*, it is possible that the inspiration for the choreography of the spectacle – with 'kar sevaks' taking down the mosque brick by brick – lay in the widely televised images of the fall of the Berlin Wall in which ordinary people taking off bits of the wall with only hand tools served to convey the idea that the act expressed democracy as such.

FASCISM AND CAPITALIST LIBERAL DEMOCRACY

Fascism always poses as democratic because it is the product of, and an intensely authoritarian reaction to, the democratization of capitalist societies. The classical fascisms – Italian fascism and German Nazism – were in an important sense the result of political crises produced by the introduction of universal franchise. But what really is fascism?

To describe any movement or government as fascist is to say that it is connected to the contradictions of capitalism. Before he led the Cold War way to equating fascism and communism as commonly 'totalitarian', the Frankfurt school theorist, Theodor Horkheimer, had clearly stated: 'He who will not speak about capitalism should keep silent about fascism too.' This is because fascism is an *exceptional* form of *capitalist* rule.

Ordinarily, that is to say when there is no extraordinary threat to the capitalist order from below or from its own crisis-generating tendencies, capitalism requires some sort of liberal and representative (rather than democratic) government. Liberal constitutions preserve the sanctity of property. Parliament is where capitalists, who normally compete with one another, can broker their common interests as a class. In the West, these liberal representative orders came to be democratized in the twentieth century as the franchise was gradually widened to become universal, thanks largely to the struggles of working people.[3] In the liberal democracies that were thus created, however, tensions between the formal popular power of democracy and the substantial inequality of capitalism remained.

They were mitigated in two major ways. On the one hand, some tensions were mitigated through the 'liberalization of democracy'– effectively its confinement to realms that did not seriously question the rule of private property – that occurred as capitalist societies were democratized.[4] On the other hand, working people won key policy concessions – particularly the welfare states and 'full employment' policies of the post-war Keynesian welfare state. This relative working-class empowerment had its equivalents outside the West in the actually existing 'Communisms' of the Eastern Bloc and the various developmental regimes of the Third World. All of them limited the rule of property in key ways that benefitted working people.

These arrangements themselves were, in one way or another, thrown into crisis and, by the 1980s, the neo-liberal New Right emerged to shift the balance of political forces once again in favour of the capitalist classes, within countries and internationally. In good part, this has been done by the hollowing out of liberal democracy itself by the increasing role of money and the media in electoral politics, the rise of a professional class of politicians, the increasing depoliticization of decision making and the rule of 'experts' (extending to the recent imposition of unelected governments in the European periphery), propaganda, corruption and voter apathy. Such compromised democracy forms the indispensable background to understanding the possibility of the re-emergence of fascism.

When the ruling class is unable to maintain power by exercising its 'hegemony'[5] through the existing political apparatus of the constitutional state and its parties, it resorts to one of several 'exceptional' forms of rule. Until the neo-liberal phase, these were usually taken to include dictatorship, which entails the outright abolition of democracy, and two others which could emerge within a formally democratic system: 'Bonapartism', an openly authoritarian form of elective rule which can arise because the contending classes are evenly matched, or fascism.[6] To these we must now add the neo-liberal hollowing out of democracy.

What distinguishes fascism from the others is that it deploys para-state organizations to impose 'order' through organized violence and intimidation. The state loses its classical 'monopoly of violence'. The personnel of these parastatal organizations for violence are typically mobilized from middle and lower-middle classes and from among the more 'lumpen' sections of the working class by arousing resentments, typically against minorities, by means of irrationalist ideologies that purport to offer easy 'final' solutions. The element of mobilization for violence makes fascism a dangerous choice for capitalist classes. While it may seem attractive as a means to reimpose order or resolve some other really or apparently critical problems, it contains the ever-present possibility that a fascist regime can act independently of the will of the ruling classes who brought it to power, as, for instance, Hitler did.[7] This is, as we shall see, very important in the Indian context, to which we now return.

THE ADVANCE OF HINDUTVA

Hindutva's violent mobilizations of the late 1980s and early 1990s paid off: the party of Hindutva, whose forward march had begun in the late 1960s and 1970s only to be interrupted by the collapse of the Janata Party and the return of Mrs Gandhi in the 1980s, resumed its rise. Having already displaced the only secular right-wing force, the Swatantra Party, decades before, the BJP now occupied the right of the political spectrum. This ensured that Right in India would be religious and communal. It also gave right-wing politics in India an interesting twist: the 'normal' party of the Right in India is also the potentially 'exceptional' (i.e., fascist) one.

This point needs to be understood before clarity can be achieved on the question of Hindutva's fascism.

The BJP advanced electorally and politically along paths cleared by neo-liberalism in the wake of economic liberalization. Though most believe that it started in the 1990s, its roots lie, as I have long argued, in the political developments of the late 1960s.[8] They polarized the polity and created a growing and increasingly clearly defined constituency for right-wing politics. Of course, as elsewhere, it could not constitute a majority, and the history of the Right in India, even more than elsewhere, given the country's poverty, must be understood as the uphill task of trying to cobble together a winning electoral coalition around its core support among the propertied. The BJP drew middle- and upper-caste and middle- and upper-class votes from the Congress. And where there was a competitor for middle-class/caste votes in the form of a regional party of the provincial propertied classes such as the Telugu Desam or the various Lok and Janata Dals, or the other sets of forces ensuring Congress decline, it allied with them in most cases.[9]

By the 1990s, the BJP was the principal opposition party in Parliament. It took power in New Delhi in coalition with regional parties in 1998 and became a contender for state power in many states, alone or in coalition with regional parties. The BJP's period in office, leading the National Democratic Alliance (NDA) coalition between 1998 and 2004, did not reopen the question of the fascism of the Sangh Parivar. Perhaps it was because the matter had been discussed relatively recently or perhaps because it was expected that the BJP's fascistic tendencies would be held in check by its coalition allies. However, the genocide of Gujarat's Muslims which was the opening act of Narendra Modi's chief ministership there is testimony that adventurist members of the Parivar could not always be restrained.

Be that as it may, the 2014 elections have put the question of fascism squarely back on the table. It is the first BJP-majority government in New Delhi headed by a prime minister who is more an RSS product than any other BJP leader so far. It was elected with the backing of the capitalist class so unified, enthusiastic and, above all, munificent, that the BJP reportedly spent more on its campaign than the ruling US president,[10] boosting its vote by a stunning 12.2 per cent compared to 2009. Though it still remained a comparatively modest 31 per cent, the magic of the first-past-the-post electoral system translated this into 52 per cent of Lok Sabha seats (282 out of 543). The question now is no longer confined to whether the RSS is a fascist movement, but extends to whether the Modi government is a fascist government.

In what follows, we first deal with the question of whether the category of fascism can be extended to instances beyond inter-war European fascisms by countering the most systematic effort to answer it in the negative. We then go on to consider the questions of the fascism of the Sangh Parivar and of the Modi government.

FASCISM: AN INTER-WAR EUROPEAN IDIOSYNCRASY?

Marshalling the long tradition of theorizing European fascism on the Left, Achin Vanaik discusses the two main possibilities that it raises: that fascism is a 'recurrent temptation' in capitalism, and that it is the result of a crisis of modernization. Vanaik rejects the second, exemplified by the ideas of Barrington Moore Jr,[11] because it considers fascism a 'revolution from above', thus failing to register the centrality of mass mobilization to fascism. We may add that it is simply impossible to understand fascism outside the context of mass democratic politics. Vanaik may, however, have considered placing the role of landed property and conservatism in mass democratic politics and the rise of fascism in a broader understanding of the evolution of the politics of the Right as the politics of property as it shifted its bases from land alone to include other capitalist property.[12]

However, Vanaik also rejected the possibility that fascism is a 'recurring temptation' in capitalist liberal democratic societies. He rejected it not only in the case of India but for the post-war world in general, concluding that 'fascism was a generic phenomenon but one which was ultimately confined spatially and temporally to inter-war

Europe'. This was far more questionable. His rejection was based on eight differences between the inter-war European context and our own times which allegedly make fascism unrepeatable: the scale of the dislocation caused by the First World War; the sense of civilizational decline and elite and popular disillusion with the liberal order; the greater receptivity to anti-liberalism and lack of confidence in bourgeois democracy; the acuity of the inter-war crisis of European capitalism; the acuteness of the subjective experience of that crisis by the capitalist class; the strength of the economic compulsions driving external expansionism of capitalist countries as theorized by the classical theories of imperialism; the much greater 'actuality of the revolution' given the greater strength and organization of the working classes and, finally, the squeezing of the middle classes.

The key to evaluating this judgement lies, perhaps, in the historical moment in which Vanaik made it. In the early 1990s, with the fall of communism in Europe and the erstwhile USSR still fresh, with the Francis Fukuyama type of triumphalism about history arriving at its capitalist liberal democratic terminus still resonating around the world, Vanaik's confidence in the stability of capitalism and the strength of liberal democracy appears at once understandable and dated. Developments since that historic moment have not borne out his confidence either in capitalism or its liberal democratic form of rule. As the neo-liberal decades wore on, they heightened the historic tensions between capitalism and democracy[13] – tensions that the Keynesian welfare state of the post-war period had, at least temporarily, lulled,[14] in good part by pulling the parties of property to the left.

In the quarter-century since the fall of European communism, capitalism has failed to overcome the 'Long Downturn' that followed its post-war 'Long Boom'. Its growth became a zero-sum game between the three major centres of capitalist accumulation[15] and became so reliant on volatile and destabilizing asset price inflation – which further worsens inequality and adds to capitalism's political legitimation difficulties – as to have no other strategy for growth – as prominent US economists both on the Right and the Left such as Larry Summers and Krugman have had to recognize recently.[16] With many emerging economies growing, by contrast, the resulting multipolarity is generating new international tensions. Politically, while the defeats inflicted on the Left and the rightward movement of many of its traditional parties have ensured the continuing dominance of neo-liberalism, it has been an economically and politically unstable dominance. This has ensured that the ability of neo-liberal right-wing parties to win elections is, if anything, less assured than it was when they were more centrist after the war. Only the hollowing out of democracy in practically all countries with the increased involvement of money and the media[17] permits right wing parties to rule in most parts of the world outside Latin America.

Europe is now home to avowedly neo-Nazi forces whose mass base has expanded thanks to the installation of unelected governments to follow the dictates of the 'troika' of the European Commission, the European Central Bank and the International Monetary Fund, not to mention the many garden variety authoritarian governments pursuing austerity. Elsewhere, as in Thailand or Egypt, we witness the remarkable spectacle of apparently popular but actually middle-class social movements demanding outright military rule. In sum, the possibilities of fascism, particularly where fascist parties and movements exist, no longer seem quite so remote. At the same time, given the deterioration of democracy under neo-liberalism, it may not seem so dramatically different from the 'new normal' of hollowed-out democracies.

While some of the differences between inter-war Europe and our own times noted by Vanaik are probably specious (when are the middle classes not being 'squeezed'? Isn't that their lot in capitalism?), others are arguably differences of degree. Undoubtedly, the background of the First World War and its cultural consequence of pervasive demoralization, the objective acuity of the economic crisis, capitalists' subjective experience of it, the novelty of universal franchise and the greater possibilities for outright colonialism differentiate the 'classical' fascisms from anything that might appear today. But they do so only by degree. They may make fascist seizures of power less fast-paced and dramatic, especially if we consider how far the deterioration of democratic processes has already advanced. In this context, the application of force and fraud to nullify democratic decisions may be hard to discern from normality. Fascism may involve forms of external aggression that must be different, given how much the international context has changed over the last century or so since the onset of the 'Thirty Years' Crisis';[18] and Western actions since the cold war certainly do not inspire democratic confidence.[19] However, these differences do not rule out the possibility of fascism today.

One difference might seem weightier and must be considered in greater detail: the 'actuality of revolution'. Certainly, compared to inter-war Europe, labour today is less organized and weaker the world over, and especially in India. However, if the occasion of fascism is provided by capitalist crises, we should remember that they can take two forms. The inter-class form – as in inter-war Europe's confrontation between a well-organized working class and a capitalist class confronted with the novelty of maintaining its rule amid mass democratic politics – is only one. The other is an intra-class form, relating to the difficulties that capitalism's inherent contradictions may generate. Even without a challenge from below, therefore, capitalist accumulation may confront problems. And when it does, as Vanaik himself acknowledges, capitalists' subjective experience of crisis is just as important as the objective details of the crisis, points that become critical below.

Ian Kershaw pointed out that a fascist movement or party 'can gain power only if the traditional elites prove incapable of controlling the mechanisms of rule, and if they are ultimately prepared to help engineer a fascist takeover and collaborate in fascist rule'[20] to regain that control. In the 2014 elections, the Indian capitalist class dumped the Congress party whose leadership of the United Progressive Alliance (UPA) had given it its best decade of growth ever[21] and steered the Indian economy relatively deftly after the 2008 financial crisis. Instead, it supported the Modi-led BJP fulsomely because, to put it in Kershaw's terms, it was frustrated at losing control over 'the mechanisms of rule' under the UPA. Indian capitalists complained long and hard about how the UPA was failing to approve key infrastructure projects fast enough, and Modi's adviser-to-be, Arvind Panagaria,[22] even obliged them by building an entire theory of what had gone wrong with economic governance in India out of those complaints.[23] Even so, the evidence for this was anything but robust.[24] What is clear is that Indian capitalists were beginning to resent even the minimal welfarist measures that were necessary to keep the Congress in power.[25] They now turned to the party that would act even more brazenly and one-sidedly in their favour. In doing this, they set their faces against the political consequences of their choice, particularly the potential of widening political opposition.

Given the weakness of labour and other forms of opposition to the ruling class, it is clear that no threat from below compelled the resort to fascism in the historical sense of driving the capitalist classes to it. But then, has it ever? Did the capitalists not have alternatives to fascism, options they chose not to exercise, even in the 'classical' European cases? Whether and to what extent the contradictions of capitalism itself led Indian capitalists to choose Modi, the BJP and the Sangh Parivar that inevitably comes with it, we can only know if the actual discussion and relations between the capitalist class and the Congress and BJP leaderships – and the concerns that led to the choice India's capitalists made – are fully documented. There is also the possibility that the resort to the fascist party was just a more attractive option for capital, one which the weakness of labour and other forms of opposition permitted because, prima facie, at least, there were fewer consequences to fear in terms of provoking disorder. Whatever the reason, the choice is potentially fateful.

SANGH PARIVAR'S FASCISM

On the question of whether the Sangh Parivar is fascist, Vanaik noted key differences, but also conceded that there were extensive similarities and that the RSS, along with a host of other movements, including in various right-wing mobilizations in Latin America or neo-Nazi organizations, could be seen as 'pre-fascist or potentially fascist'.[26] The reason was that, for Vanaik, the threat of fascism is best seen as dwelling in not this or that movement, but in the larger situation:

> The 'logic' or 'principal dynamics' of fascism ... is never the result of the evolution of some 'organism' [or movement] marked by its infant or adolescent or even adult characteristics as irremediably fascist. The fascist minimum [i.e., the minimally fascist situation] is always the complex structuration of characteristics both internal and external to the 'fascist protagonist' in a given context. The external or contextual or 'shaping' factors are more important than any 'inner logic' or 'essence' of the putative 'fascist organism'. It is the fascist situation that 'matures', not the fascist entity.[27]

If by this Vanaik means only that many fascist movements might never come to power, he would be right. But does that make the movements that do not come to power simply 'pre-fascist'? In attempting to dismiss the possibility that movements can be judged as fascist independently of whether they come to power or not, he appears to be taking the untenable, if not impractical, position that one can only designate a movement fascist retrospectively. A fascist regime presupposes the availability of the fascist option and that can only be provided by a fascist movement. This is why the question of whether the Sangh Parivar is fascist must be considered.

Writers who consider the Sangh Parivar fascist, as well as some who don't, have remarked that it has been in existence for a long time whereas the classical fascist and Nazi parties were relatively new when they came to power. However, this is simply because the classical instances of fascism occurred when the combination of capitalism with mass democratic politics, which forms the political ground on which alone fascist seeds could germinate, was itself quite recent.

Many scholars baulk at applying the label fascist to any contemporary phenomenon because of the sheer enormity of Nazism's consequences. Vanaik, for instance, worries that 'For a Marxist to believe that the forces of Hindu nationalism embody the threat of an Indian fascism is to give the present struggle against it something more than an exceptional gravitas. It is to give it, centrally and inescapably, an apocalyptic charge'.[28] However, as Hobsbawm points out, had fascism not triumphed in Germany, it would not have been so consequential.[29] Moreover, as we have already pointed out, in our own time, given the already advanced deterioration of democracy, the transition to fascism is liable to appear considerably less dramatic.

Christophe Jaffrelot's discussion of the RSS and the question of its fascism is arguably the most systematic to date. He identified three differences between the RSS and the classical fascist parties which prevented him from designating the RSS fascist. He found, on the basis of detailed examination of the works of the organization's founders, that 'the supreme concept in the RSS's doctrine is not race but society'. Secondly, while the two European movements sought to capture the state and use it to advance their ideology, 'the RSS ... is not a putschist organization and Golwalkar considered Hitler's capture of the state a mistake'. Finally, the RSS was distinctive in emphasizing organization over a 'supreme leader'.[30] All three are easily disposed of.

Jaffrelot's tediously earnest discussions of the founding ideas of Hindutva's ideologues and how they compare with fascism are entirely beside the point. What Hobsbawm noted about fascism's intellectual character certainly applies to Hindutva:

Theory was not the strong point of movements devoted to the inadequacy of reason and rationalism and the superiority of instinct and will. ... Hostile as it was on principle to the heritage of the eighteenth-century enlightenment and the French revolution, fascism could not formally believe in modernity and progress, but it had no difficulty in combining a lunatic set of beliefs with technological modernity in practical matters, except where it crippled its basic scientific research on ideological grounds ... It also provided the proof that men can, without difficulty, combine crack-brained beliefs about the world with a confident mastery of contemporary high technology. The late twentieth century, with its fundamentalist sects wielding the weapons of television and computer-programmed fund-raising, has made us familiar with this phenomenon.[31]

Jaffrelot's understanding of European fascisms, being a largely liberal one, is under-theorized while his reading of the texts and history of the RSS is simply ahistorical and decontextualized. Jaffrelot's objection that the RSS concept of the 'other' is not based on 'race' is confused on several levels. Firstly, Jaffrelot would have to show that 'race' was essential to fascism, which he cannot.[32] Secondly, given the diversity of peoples who have come to inhabit the subcontinent, and its criss-crossing divisions of caste, language, religion and ethnicity, no 'othering' based on 'race' could possibly work. Any theoretically serious inquiry into whether the Sangh Parivar was fascist would have to look for functional substitutes. In Hindutva's case, the most important of these is the 'othering' of India's, and the subcontinent's, Muslims with important borrowings from the West's Islamophobia of recent decades.

Jaffrelot's second argument simply fails to take note of the RSS's tendency to stay on the colonial British government's good side: to claim that they sought to control the state under a colonial regime would have simply invited colonial-grade repression. As for the RSS's emphasis on organization, it was something which also characterized European fascisms. If one of the essential traits of fascism is to offer the ruling class access to an organization capable of imposing order and/or performing other tasks above and beyond what the normal state apparatus was capable of doing or constitutionally permitted to do, organization was essential. That it is hardly incompatible with a personality cult – whether in the case of Hitler, Mussolini or Modi – may be clearer now in the Indian case than it was before. But it was never unclear.

Schematic discussions like Jaffrelot's are really not good guides for judging the question of the Sangh Parivar's fascism. A historical view is necessary and it would begin by acknowledging that the classical fascisms were part of a broader resurgence of the Right in inter-war Europe which included traditional conservatives, an anti-liberal corporatist Right and the religious Right.[33] The parallel with the New Right of our own time – neo-liberal but never unmixed with cultural and socially authoritarian themes[34] – need not be belaboured. As in inter-war Europe, within this broader rise of the Right, various strands of right-wing politics, including the established liberal and conservative parties of the Right, mingled. The oft-invoked opposition between conservatism and fascism, while not without its uses in distinguishing between the aristocratic bases of the former and the plebeian origins of the latter, can be overblown. There was never an unbridgeable divide between them. Conservatives and even liberals may have been contemptuous of the lower socio-economic origins of fascists but when it was necessary to retain political purchase on fast-changing contexts of political crises, they were quite ready to ally with fascism, even without holding the proverbial nose.[35] Similarly, it is well known that the religious Right was not averse to allying with the otherwise self-consciously pagan fascism. While conservatism is no longer a major component of the Right, a similar intermingling between the neo-liberal and the communal and fascist Right can be witnessed in our own time, and not only in India.[36]

Finally, the social basis of fascism is not at all dissimilar from the social strata that Hindutva mobilizes as part of its core support:

> The common element of [the classical fascist] movements was the resentment of little men in a society that crushed them between the rock of big business on one side and the hard place of rising mass labour movements on the other. Or which, at the very least, deprived them of the respectable position they had occupied in the social order, and believed to be their due, or the social status in a dynamic society to which they felt they had a right to aspire.[37]

This middle and lower-middle strata formed the core of fascism's social base, though elements of the labouring poor could also be mobilized.[38] In our own time, this core has been expanded by the professional middle classes – whom Nicos Poulantzas, the Greek–French Marxist, called the New Petty Bourgeoisie. Harold Perkins pointed out long ago that those among this group employed by corporations tended to vote for right-wing parties and those who were employed by the state or NGOs tended to vote for left-of-centre parties.[39] He forgot to add that they were also responsible for shifting Left parties themselves to the Right, as exemplified classically, in Britain, by Tony Blair and his New Labour. In India, the parallel is with the Congress's own rightward shift. The more recent rise of the Aam Aadmi Party (AAP), made up of 'social movement activists' as well as an array of small and big capitalists, with its ambiguity about Hindutva is another analogous development. The expanded middle classes of the old and new petty bourgeoisies are everywhere the social bases for right-wing politics, including its more authoritarian and/or fascist forms.

Moreover, since the last time the question of the fascism of the Sangh Parivar was seriously considered by scholars of Hindutva, Marzia Casolari has established that '(a) the main historical organizations and leaders of Hindu nationalism had a distinctive and sustained interest in fascism and Nazism; (b) fascist ideological influences on Hindu nationalism were present and relevant; and (c) to a certain extent, these influences were channeled through direct contacts between Hindu nationalists and members of the Italian fascist state.'[40]

THE MODI GOVERNMENT'S FASCISM

If the Sangh Parivar is a fascist organization, if the BJP majority government has assumed office with capitalist backing more fulsome than any previous Indian government, if a cult of personality and 'decisionism'[41] surround Modi as no previous Indian leader, if RSS cadres have campaigned for Modi on a scale and with a zeal they never showed any other BJP leader, it follows that a fascist government is in power in New Delhi. Whether it is an 'optional' fascism or a 'necessary' one depends on whether the Indian capitalist class chose Modi and the BJP because they simply could not get on without them, or felt they could not so get on, or simply because they preferred the BJP. The question is complicated by the fact that the BJP is both the 'normal' part of the Right and its fascist party. If the consequences appear less dire, it is as much because of the worldwide deterioration of democracy in general, and in India in particular.

It remains to be seen to what extent the Modi government will deploy, or have to deploy (two very different things), its shock troops in the maintenance of order and thus demonstrate its distinctiveness as a fascist government. Certainly, fascistic offences are not hard to find in its barely year-and-a-half-old tenure: the appointment of Parivar personnel to key positions of state and in the cultural and education sector, the persecution of activists, the violence against minorities for electoral and general mobilizational purposes, rising tensions on the border with Pakistan, secret deals with foreign companies, a legislative programme designed exclusively to please India's corporate sector, attacks on environmental and labour/pro-poor legislation and programmes, the list could go on. Perhaps it is for those who would like to argue that the government is not fascist to explain why they continue to think so.

It is true that in India with its everyday police brutality, judicial malfeasance and executive and legislative corruption, unconstitutional and illegal political activity is rife. However, it still makes a difference whether violations of the law and the Constitution and the general turn towards authoritarianism are undertaken 'pragmatically' or 'programmatically'.

A final similarity to fascism concerns contradiction and, therefore, dynamics. Class rule is always contradictory and exceptional forms have historically been fatefully so. The capitalists who backed Modi so enthusiastically may yet find that he cannot restore their political control; and that, to adapt Kershaw's apt formulation about the Nazi regime to contemporary India:

> ... the autonomy of [Modi's] leadership expands rather than contracts, and with it the scope for implementation of the central tenets of the 'political religion' [in Modi's case, Hindutva] which forms the raison d'être and action-target of the [Hindutva] movement. Instead of restoring their own control, the traditional [i.e., capitalist] elites then find themselves outflanked and tend to adopt high-risk policies which place the reproduction of their own continued dominance in jeopardy.[42]

Classically, the high-risk strategy of the German capitalists was military expansionism. Certainly, external aggression in some form cannot be ruled out. The BJP is, after all, the party of Pokhran-II and seeks to project Indian power among its immediate neighbours and in the wider region[43] with its conception of 'Akhand Bharat'. Those who thought Modi's invitation to the heads of government in the neighbourhood to attend his swearing-in as prime minister was some sort of goodwill gesture might think again; it was more like the holding of an imperial durbar at which subordinate princes are invited to pay obeisance. But even short of external aggression, there is no shortage of domestic high-risk strategies: excessively zealous repression and persecution of Opposition forces and minorities and, of course, implementation of Hindutva's 'core agenda' – a uniform civil code attacking the country's Muslim minority; abrogation of Article 370 of the Indian Constitution giving special status to Jammu and Kashmir, the Union's only Muslim-majority state; and construction of a Ram temple at the site of Babri Masjid in Ayodhya still disputed by Muslims.[44] Any and all of these can be guaranteed to result in acute political problems and/or considerable violence, with or without external implications. When such external and/or internal high-risk strategies are pursued, will the capitalist class be able to dump their man and the movement behind him? After all, who rides the tiger dare not dismount. What will the consequences be? Such questions indicate the grave dangers in which India's capitalists have landed the country by supporting Modi.

NOTES

1 See pre-eminently Ahmad 1993, Patnaik 1993 and Sarkar 1993.

2 Ahmad 1993: 22.

3 Geoff Eley 2003.

4 MacPherson 1992.

5 As Gramsci called it, though see Anderson 1976 for the problems of using this concept to describe relations between antagonistic classes.

6 Poulantzas 1970: 11.

7 Kershaw 1989.

8 Desai 1999; see also Desai 2008.

9 I discuss the underlying logic and dynamics of the BJP's advance and alliances in Desai 2004a, 2004b, 2004c, 2010 and 2014 and its differential geography in my writings on Gujarat, especially Desai 2011.

10 Varadarajan 2014.

11 Moore Jr, 1966.

12 Desai 2004a and 2006.

13 MacPherson 1992 is a classical study of these.

14 Crouch 2012.

15 Brenner 1998.

16 Larry Summers (2013) and Krugman (2012)

17 Mair 2006 and 2013.

18 See Desai 2013.

19 Pilger 2015.

20 Kershaw 1989.

21 Nagraj 2013.

22 Arvind Panagaria 2014.

23 The parallels with Carl Schmitt providing the legal justification for Hitler's seizure of power via similar theory production out of hot air cannot be ignored. See Desai 2011.

24 Ghatak et al., 2014.

25 Desai 2004, 2010.

26 Vanaik 1994: 1739.

27 Ibid.

28 Ibid.: 1743.

29 Hobsbawm 1994: 116–17.

30 Jaffrelot 1993: 61–2.

31 Hobsbawm 1994: 117 and 118.

32 Ibid.: 117.

33 Hobsbawm 1994: 112–15.

34 Desai 2006 and 2009.

35 Blinkhorn 1990.

36 Desai 2004a and 2006.

37 Hobsbawm 1994: 119.

38 Ibid.: 117.

39 Harold Perkins, 1989.

40 Marzia Casolari, 2000.

41 Desai 2001.

42 Kershaw 1989: 57–58.

43 Desai 2002.

44 Noorani 2014.

REFERENCES

Ahmad, Aijaz. 1993. 'Culture, Community, Nation: On the Ruins of Ayodhya', *Social Scientist*, July-August, Vol. 21: Nos. 7–8.

Anderson, Perry. 1976. 'The Antinomies of Antonio Gramsci', *New Left Review* I/100, November-December, pp. 5–78.

Blinkhorn, Martin (ed.). 1990. *Fascists and Conservatives: The Radical Right and the Establishment in the Twentieth Century*, London: Routledge.

Brenner, Robert. 1998. 'The Economics of Global Turbulence', *New Left Review* I/229, May-June: 1-265.

Casolari, Marzia. 2000. 'Hindutva's foreign tie-up in the 1930s: Archival Evidence', *Economic and Political Weekly*, 22 January, pp. 218–28.

Crouch, Colin. 2012. 'Democracy and Capitalism in the Wake of the Financial Crisis', in Kate Nash, Alan Scott and Edwin Amenta (eds), *Wiley-Blackwell Companion to Political Sociology*, London: Blackwell.

Desai, Radhika. 1999. 'Culturalism and the Contemporary Right: the Indian Bourgeoisie and Political Hindutva', *Economic and Political Weekly*, Vol. XXXIV, no. 12, 20 March, pp. 695–712

——. 2001. 'Fetishizing Phantoms: Carl Schmitt, Chantal Mouffe and "The Political". Abbie Bakan and Eleanor MacDonald (eds), *Critical Political Studies: Debates and Dialogues from the Left*, Montreal: McGill-Queen's Press, pp. 387–408.

——. 2002. 'Tryst with Fate: India and Pakistan in the War on Terrorism', *Economic and Political Weekly*, Vol. XXXVII, No. 33, 17 August.

——. 2004a. *Slouching Towards Ayodhya: From Congress to Hindutva in Indian Politics*, Second Revised Edition, Three Essays: New Delhi.

——. 2004b. 'Forward March of Hindutva Halted?', *New Left Review* 30, second series, November-December 2004, pp. 49–67. Reprinted in Arvind Sivaramakrishnan, *Short on Democracy: Issues Facing Indian Political Parties*, Imprint One: New Delhi, 2007.

——. 2004c. 'The Cast(e) of Anti-Secularism', in Mushirul Hasan (ed.), *Will Secular India Survive?*, Imprint One, New Delhi, pp. 175–209.

——. 2006. 'Neo-Liberalism and Cultural Nationalism: A *Danse Macabre*', in Dieter Plehwe, Bernhard Walpen and Gisela Nuenhoeffer (eds), *Neo-Liberal Hegemony: A Global Critique*, New York: Routledge, pp. 222–235.

——. 2008. 'Die Gegenrevolution im Zeitlupentempo: Von Entwicklungsstaat bis Neoliberalen Staat in Indien', in Ingo Schmidt (ed.), *Die Heimatfronten der Globalisierung: Nationale Klassenkompromisse, Neuzusammensetzung des Proletariats und Transnationale Opposition*, Berlin: VSA Verlag. English version available upon request.

——. 2009. *Developmental and Cultural Nationalisms*, London: Routledge.

——. 2010. 'Hindutva's Ebbing Tide?', Sanjay Ruparelia, Stuart Corbridge, John Harriss and Sanjaya Reddy (eds), *Great Transformations*, New York: Routledge, pp. 172–185.

——. 2011. 'Gujarat's Hindutva of Capitalist Development', *South Asia*, Vol. XXXIV, no. 3, December, pp. 354–381

——. 2013. *Geopolitical Economy: After US Hegemony, Globalization and Empire*, London: Pluto Press. The Future of World Capitalism book series.

——. 2014. 'A Latter-Day Fascism?', *Economic and Political Weekly*, 30 August, Volume XLIX, no. 35, pp. 48–58.

Eley, Geoffrey. 2003. *Forging Democracy: The History of the Left in Europe 1850–2000*, Oxford: Oxford University Press.

Fukuyama, Francis. 1989. 'The End of History', *The National Interest*, Summer.

Hobsbawm, Eric. 1994. *Age of Extremes: The Short Twentieth Century, 1914–1991*, London: Michael Joseph.

Maitreesh Ghatak, Parikshit Ghosh and Ashok Kotwal. 2014. 'Growth in the Time of the UPA', *Economic & Political Weekly*, 19 April.

Jaffrelot, Christophe. 1993. *The Hindu Phenomenon*, New Delhi: Viking.

Kershaw, Ian. 1989. 'The Nazi State: An Exceptional State?', *New Left Review* I/ 176, July-August.

Krugman, Paul. 2012. *New York Times*, blog, 16 November 2012. http:// krugman.blogs.nytimes.com/2013/11/16/secular-stagnation-coalmines-bubbles-and-larry-summers/?_php=true&_type=blogs&_r=0 Accessed 18 March 2014.

MacPherson, Crawford B. 1992. *The Real World of Democracy*, Toronto: House of Anansi Press.

Mair, Peter. 2006. 'Ruling the Void: The Hollowing of Western Democracy', *New Left Review* II/42, November-December.

_____. 2013. *Ruling the Void: The Hollowing of Western Democracy*, London: Verso.

Moore Jnr, Barrington, 1966. *Social Origins of Dictatorship and Democracy*, Boston: Beacon Press.

Nagraj, R. 2013. 'India's Dream Run, 2003–8: Understanding the Boom and its Aftermath', *Economic and Political Weekly*, Vol. XLVIII, no. 20, pp. 39–51.

Noorani, A.G. 2014. 'An Impossible Agenda', *Frontline*, 11 June.

Panagariya, Arvind. 'The Promise of Modinomics', 10 June 2014, http://www. foreignaffairs.com/articles/141556/arvind-panagariya/the-promise-of-modinomics accessed on 28 June 2014.

Patnaik, Prabhat. 1993. 'The Fascism of Our Times', *Social Scientist*, vol. 21, no. 3–4, 1993.

Perkin, Harold. 1989. *The Rise of Professional Society*, London: Cape.

Pilger, John. 2015. 'Why the Rise of Fascism is the Issue', *Counterpunch*, 27 February, http://www.counterpunch.org/2015/02/27/why-the-rise-of-fascism-is-again-the-issue/

Poulantzas, Nicos. 1970. *Fascism and Dictatorship*, London: New Left Books.

Prashad, Vijay. 1996. 'Emergency Assessments', *Social Scientist*, vol. 24, no. 280–81 (September-October), pp. 36–68.

Sarkar, Sumit. 1993. 'The Fascism of the Sangh Parivar', *Economic and Political Weekly*, 30 January.

Summers, Larry. 2013. Speech at the IMF's Fourteenth Annual Research Conference in Honour of Stanley Fischer. 8 November. http://larrysummers.com/imf-fourteenth-annual-research-conference-in-honor-of-stanley-fischer/. Accessed on 18 March 2014.

Therborn, Göran. 1977. 'The Rule of Capital and The Rise of Democracy', *New Left Review* I/103, May-June.

Vanaik, Achin. 1994. 'Situating the Threat of Hindu Nationalism: Problems with the Fascist Paradigm', *Economic and Political Weekly*, 9 July.

Varadarajan, Siddharth. 2014. 'The Best Democracy Money Can Buy', *The Economic Times*, 30 April.

Who Is the Real Narendra Modi: A 'Communal Czar' or an 'Inclusive Icon'?

R. Jagannathan

~~∀~~

R. Jagannathan is former editor-in-chief of *Forbes India*. One of India's leading commentators on politics and economy, he has previously headed firstpost.com, *Business Today*, *Business World*, *Financial Express* and *DNA* newspaper.

Narendra Modi has disappointed many people. He has disappointed his vocal supporters by proving to be less right-wing – economically or culturally – than they thought he was. But he has disappointed his foes even more by refusing to live up to their preferred image of him as the chief minister who presided over a communal carnage in Gujarat in 2002. They are thus reduced to criticizing him indirectly by focusing on some of the outrageously bigoted comments of fringe elements of the Sangh Parivar, a parivar that Modi has been an intrinsic part of for nearly half a century.

The truth is Narendra Damodardas Modi, the first political leader in thirty years to win a full parliamentary majority after Rajiv Gandhi in 1984, is defying the stereotypes. He is neither the Ronald Reagan nor the Margaret Thatcher that the economic Right hoped he would be; but he isn't the Hindu icon that the cultural and religious Right would have liked him to be. A Ram Mandir in Ayodhya will certainly not be on his to-do list. He would see that as a needless distraction.

Power moderates politicians. Just as Emperor Akbar started out as a semi-bigot but turned out to be an early examplar of plurality during his reign, Modi has left Gujarat 2002 far behind. He is charting his own path to political longevity, creating a trajectory that would put his Bharatiya Janata Party bang in the centre of the political spectrum. Even if you grant him a centre-right orientation, he cannot be termed right-wing in any conventional sense of the term as understood in the West, or by the English-speaking elite in 'liberal, secular' India.

So what really does Modi stand for? What is he like as a person as opposed to his airbrushed image? What does he really believe in as opposed to what he has said after becoming prime minister of India? What is his economics about? Does he subscribe to the Sangh agenda of India being a Hindu nation, or has he left even that behind? How exactly does he view minorities? Is his campaign slogan – 'Sabka Saath, Sabka Vikas' – a genuinely non-discriminatory approach to development, or a cover for not addressing the real deprivations faced by some minority communities in India, especially Muslims.

Short of putting him on the couch, it is unlikely that we will get very clear answers to these questions. But one can reconstruct the real Narendra Modi from the fragments of himself he presents to us on various well-chosen public occasions, and especially his foreign tours, where he seems to show more of his personal self than he does in India. At home, he always seems serious, suggesting to everyone that he is all about work and no play. Abroad, whether playing drums in Japan or taking 'selfies' with Chinese Prime Minister Li Keqiang or counterparts in Mongolia or Australia, he seems more willing to let his hair down. The fun-loving Modi emerges. But, for some reason, he does not want to be seen this way by Indians. Here he is the 56-inch chest macho man, who works 24×7 without a break for his people.

Politically, he has many sides to him: He can be the combative verbal brawler who is willing to mock Sonia Gandhi's Italian origins, or indulge in subtle anti-minority innuendo by referring to the Congress party as the Delhi Sultanate, or Rahul Gandhi as 'Shehzada'. He can be cutting in his lampooning of Sonia's 'damaad', son-in-law Robert Vadra, a man with an acquisitive streak in property and land deals. But once the battle is over, he is the dutiful son, seeking his mother's blessing. After an electoral victory, he is all humility and propriety. After the Gujarat election win in 2012, he personally visited his bête noire and former party rival, Keshubhai Patel, and sought his goodwill. After his Lok Sabha victory, he personally visited Manmohan Singh at his new home. No protocol stood in the way of this show of respect to a former prime minister.

Clearly, Modi has many sides to his persona – his public one and his private one. While we may never know all there is to know about the real Narendra Modi, we do know one thing: how he is seen by the public at large is really, really important to him. That is the first clue to his real persona. He wants control over his image, and how he is seen.

This is what explains his refusal to engage with the media in open-ended Q&A sessions or free-for-all press conferences. He does not want to be surprised by unexpectedly embarrassing questions. To be sure, this strategy is not unique to Modi. It has been deployed successfully by many Indian politicians – Sonia and Rahul Gandhi, J. Jayalalithaa of the All-India Anna Dravida Munnetra Kazhagam (AIADMK), Mayawati of the Bahujan Samaj Party (BSP), or even Naveen Patnaik of the Biju Janata Dal (BJD). They do this both to preserve an aura of mystery around themselves, which keeps media interest in them alive most of the time, but also to avoid having to answer tough questions.

This strategy has been honed to perfection by Bollywood celebrities. The big stars refuse to talk one-on-one to anyone till there is some film that's about to be released. Then they are willing to talk to all journalists who can be trusted to focus their questions on areas that the stars are happy to talk about. Their forthcoming films then get just the kind of free publicity that money cannot buy.

Modi used the Bollywood star strategy extremely well in the run-up to the 2014 Lok Sabha elections, when he declined all requests for one-on-one interviews till the elections were well under way in mid-April. Then, bang, Modi gave a well-choreographed interview, complete with regular chants of 'Modi, Modi' by his audience, in Rajat Sharma's *Aap ki Adalat*. Modi got the media he wanted – just when he wanted it to serve his purpose. At other times, he is off-bounds for the media.

This brings us to a second insight: Modi wants to be liked. It is, of course, entirely human to want to be liked, but Modi seems to need adulation a bit more than most of us. Modi is at his best when he has an audience that likes him. Hence his preference for controlled interactions as opposed to uncontrollable pressers in front of the national and international media. Modi fears humiliation in public like the plague.

To be sure, there is no getting away from the vitriolic pens of his critics, audience or no audience. To combat this, Modi has a simple strategy to deal with his regular critics: ignore them. He knows that relentless criticism tends to blunt the credibility of those who dislike him. They thus serve to enhance his appeal with those who would like to believe in him. This is what pushed middle-class India to ignore his critics despite their endless attacks on him about 2002.

Modi's transformation from the Communal Czar of 2002 to the Inclusive Icon of 2014 once again underlines the importance Modi attaches to managing perceptions. Consider how he has repackaged himself continuously. In 2002, as an unknown politician emerging from the shadows of the Sangh Parivar, he needed an issue to catapult him to leader and vote winner. The Godhra train burning incident gave him the opportunity. While the jury is out on whether he did enough to stop the communal killings or even covertly encouraged them, there is little doubt that 2002 was key to his emergence as undisputed leader of the BJP in Gujarat.

But once in power, he had less use for this polarizing persona. And, over the next few years, Modi saw his 2002 image as a trap. The Vishwa Hindu Parishad and Sangh hotheads were sidelined, and shown who's boss. They slithered out of the state. Modi decided that this image needed reinvention, and he consciously adopted development and growth as his calling cards. He organized the Vibrant Gujarat Summit, where the world's businessmen congregated to celebrate Gujarat's unique business-friendliness and sing praises of the state's leader. The Gujarat model then became his route to fame. It was also his stepping stone to the national stage.

But all talk of the Gujarat model has stopped now that he is prime minister. Gone is his overt business-friendliness, or his open door to businessmen. Modi in his third avatar, as prime minister, is talking about poverty, inclusive growth, stopping open defecation, and women's safety, less about being business-friendly. In fact, he talks poverty at home, and business abroad. Indian businessmen, who were raucously pro-Modi till last year, are now muttering darkly about the slow pace of change on the ground. Not that they have stopped believing in him altogether; it's just that they have realized that there is a new Modi in the works. It is the Modi they did not know as chief minister of Gujarat.

This offers another key insight: Modi has a strong aversion to being seen as anybody's pawn. One of the big falsehoods built up around Modi by his political rivals is that he favours business cronies, with Gautam Adani and Mukesh Ambani being mentioned repeatedly as examples of such cronyism. The crackdown against lobbyists in early 2015, which led to the arrests of several employees and power brokers linked to big business houses for allegedly being in possession of sensitive documents, was intended to put the fear of God into them. Modi does not like being controlled by anybody, least of all big business.

Even in politics he tends not to have any full-time buddies. He is a political and emotional loner. Even though Finance Minister Arun Jaitley and party president Amit Shah are said to be his close confidants, the bare fact may be simpler: their alleged closeness to Modi is evidence that he currently needs them for his purposes. They do not necessarily carry too much personal clout with him, though they may like to give everyone that impression.

Anyone looking for an answer to the question of what Modi really is about, should start from this possibility: he does not like to be vulnerable to anyone or to any accusation. And, this is why he chooses his image to match the requirements of his political and personal goals.

This does not mean he has no core beliefs. One of the things he really believes in is a sense of Indianness that has a Hindu core, but practical politics in a fractious polity will prevent him from talking too much about his Hindu leanings. Instead, he will talk in Hindi to emphasize his cultural rootedness, and tends to use projects with quasi-religious names and symbolism to send out subtle messages on this front. The project to clean the Ganga, for example, is named *Namami Gange*. His choice of Swami Vivekananda as his personal inspirational icon is an important signal of how he wants to be seen in some circles – Hindu but not overtly so.

Modi probably also shares the Sangh Parivar's anti-Nehru sensibility. In the Sangh view, Nehru was essentially anti-Hindu, but Modi will not make any such suggestion directly. He will instead try to cut the Nehruvian ethos down to size by emphasizing Gandhi, Patel and, of course, Deendayal Upadhyay, who have obvious Hindu cultural credentials, in contrast to Nehru's Western value systems. Even in his choice of using Muslim icons to woo the minorities, he will choose non-controversial heroes. Among them: Dara Shikoh, the man whom Aurangzeb the bigot killed to capture the throne; Abbas Tyabji, leader of the salt satyagraha; and Unani scholar Hakim Ajmal Khan. Some of the Modi government's schemes or events intended to woo minorities carry these names, sending the subtle message that he can care for minorities without pandering to minority-ism and embracing identity politics.

Another key ingredient in the Modi persona is a strong sense of destiny about his own role in building India. His speeches talk about himself and his dreams of India, leading critics to point out that he is all about 'I, me, myself'. But his achievement orientation is entwined in this 'I' obsession. Modi would like to be seen as India's best prime minister, the man who removed poverty and made India a great power. This dream caters to all his core support bases: the Hindu pride brigade and the aspirational middle classes who dream of a better life and a more muscular Indian presence in the comity of nations. The non-resident Indian diaspora is most vocal in this articulation, as a strong India both enhances their own identity and allows them greater respect in the countries they have chosen to make their fortunes in. Modi's biggest successes relate to his able projection of India abroad.

The world sees a rising India in Modi, but what it would like to know most about Modi is what his business beliefs are. Is he the free marketer that many foreign businessmen saw in him when he was chief minister of Gujarat? What is his vision on the role of government in business and the economy? Will he cut government down to size or expand it? Before his election, his most quoted statements were the following two. One, 'government has no business to be in business', and two, 'minimum government, maximum governance'.

The two statements, made both before he was elected prime minister and repeated by him before business audiences, are not actually what they seem to imply. They do not imply that Modi is going to shrink government like a Reagan, or be a Thatcher by aggressively selling off state assets. They are a broad statement of intent meaning the following: one, government will largely be supportive of business by focusing on making ease of business its goal; and two, selling state assets will not be a priority, but a fair-weather proposition, when politically feasible or necessary to cut the fiscal deficit.

Not once has Modi suggested he is going to privatize anything; nor has he said that government is going to recede into the background, allowing free market forces to bring economic growth. Modi actually believes in making public sector companies autonomous and efficient; he has no doctrinal belief in privatization. This is why he is hesitant even to privatize minor banks badly in need of capital. He will only sell companies that are beyond hope of revival.

His most important statement on his economic and social vision was made at a global business summit in January 2015, where he said: 'The government must nurture an ecosystem where the economy is primed for growth; and growth promotes all-round development; where development is employment-generating; and employment is enabled by skills; where skills are synced with production; and production is benchmarked to quality; where quality meets global standards; and meeting global standards drives prosperity. Most importantly, this prosperity is for the welfare of all.'[1]

He also enunciated his vision for the state and its role. He saw the state as useful in five areas: 'The first is public goods such as defence, police, and judiciary. The second is externalities which hurt others, such as pollution. For this, we need a regulatory system. The third is market power; where monopolies need controls. The fourth is information gaps; where you need someone to ensure that medicines are genuine and so on. Last, we need a well-designed welfare and subsidy mechanism to ensure that the bottom of society is protected from deprivation. This specially includes education and health care. In the five areas where we need government, we require competent, efficient and non-corrupt arms of government. We in government must constantly ask the question: How much money am I spending, and what outcomes am I getting in return? For this, government agencies have to be improved to become competent.'

Modi wants government to be more efficient, and will not necessarily shrink it. His vision for the state is probably bound up with his own political vision and his lead role in it.

Pratap Bhanu Mehta, president of the Centre for Policy Research, perhaps summarizes best the enigma that is Modi. He wrote in *The Indian Express*: 'He is hard to grasp because he is the product of a peculiarly contradictory moment in Indian democracy. He is a centraliser who looms large. A sense of his self is infused in every speech. Some yearned for exactly this kind of leader. But his sense of self-legitimation also draws power from democracy: an architect of his own fortune, who represents, in his own way, a deepening vernacularisation of democracy.'[2]

Mehta's conclusion leaves us with a question mark: 'He is seeking legitimacy in the eyes of the people: the compulsive *desire* to project an image is in service of this goal. But it also means that he will don different costumes, languages and even headgear when necessary. The script will evolve as he reads the people.'

Put another way, what you see is what Modi wants you to see. The rest is pure conjecture.

NOTES

1   Read the speech here: http://www.narendramodi.in/economic-times-global-business-summit.

2   'The Elusive Modi', 26 May 2015, http://indianexpress.com/article/opinion/columns/the elusive-modi.

The Rediscovery of India

Faisal Devji

꙰

Dr Faisal Devji is reader in modern South Asian history and fellow of St Antony's College at the University of Oxford, where he is also director of the Asian Studies Centre.

While it is clear that Narendra Modi has brought a new style of leadership to Indian politics, and that his party has a new vision for the country, this project is at the same time enmeshed in practices and institutions inherited from the past. It has been noticed by many, for example, that a number of the prime minister's most publicized initiatives, from the active role he plays on the international stage to his direct links with the bureaucracy and focus on collective hygiene, cannot but follow precedents set, respectively, by Jawaharlal Nehru, Indira Gandhi and even by the Mahatma himself. In what way, then, does the new government represent India's past, much of it associated with a party and politics that Mr Modi is strongly meant to oppose, and how might it extricate itself from this received history? I will explore this question here by reflecting on three important themes by which the Bharatiya Janata Party (BJP) and its leader are known: nationalism, party politics and governance.

PSEUDO-SECULAR

One of the peculiarities of Indian political debate is that everyone claims to be secular while accusing others of not being so. Secularism's hegemony as an idea was made clear by former BJP president, L.K. Advani, when he coined the now famous term 'pseudo-secular' to describe his political opponents. But if secularism is so dominant an idea, this is because it is and has always been deployed as a polemical category as much as a constitutional principle, and indeed its insertion, along with socialism, in the Constitution by Indira Gandhi was itself a partisan act. In colonial times, for example, Congressmen identified secularism with nationalism, which was in turn held to be the real antonym of communalism. In other words, it was the pluralism and popularity of Congress, compared with the supposedly sectarian appeal of Hindu and Muslim parties, that were seen as defining its secular credentials, and this in a demographic rather than constitutional way.

Since Independence, however, secularism has increasingly been opposed to communalism, with the nation no longer central to its definition. Is it, therefore, being separated from a strictly populist logic to assume a purely juridical character? This might well indicate the nation's failure to demonstrate its plurality, and therefore also its secularism. And so the latter must instead be sought in the pre-modern past, or identified with particular traditions such as that of Hinduism. Even in the days of its alleged dominance under Nehru, secularism could hardly be said to possess its own history or even existential reality, given that its membership included both the religious and irreligious. Indeed, secularists had to lay claim to explicitly religious precedents, such as bhakti or Sufi forms of devotion, and the pluralistic festivals with which these were often associated. In other words, their condescending reference was invariably to the 'folk' devotions that had never, in fact, been part of the 'culture' of such self-professed secularists.

Both Congress and the BJP continue to invoke a populist and indeed majoritarian logic to define the secular, but the changing nature of the Indian polity has given this rhetoric a quite different meaning. For the folk elements that had characterized nationalist visions of a mixed culture, including bhakti and Sufi literary forms, have been replaced by varieties of ostensibly high-culture religiosity that no longer need to display any pluralism, as long as they are assumed to be 'tolerant', a term that in the nationalist past had been used for another kind of high culture, that of imperial rulers like Ashoka or Akbar. Nehru himself preferred this form of the secular, which also served as a historical mask for Congress's quasi-imperial vision of itself. Before Independence, after all, its claims to hold the demographic middle ground between religious extremes had mirrored British attempts to constitute the colonial state as a neutral third party between Hindus and Muslims, itself a classically liberal position, despite the fact that it was deployed in an illiberal political system.

By making such a claim while not yet in control of the state, Congress signalled its intention of taking it over, and in the meantime creating an alternative structure of authority in Indian society. But like the colonial state and its inappropriately liberal model of rule, Congress also sought to delimit the political arena by circumscribing it within certain linguistic and institutional conventions, thus depoliticizing everything outside these as 'irrational', 'superstitious' and the like. And yet it was this very Congress, especially under Gandhi's influence, that had always subjected the 'neutrality' of British rule, conceived as the impartiality of a third party situated between Hindus and Muslims, to criticism by describing it as a form of 'divide and rule'. What did it mean, then, to claim a neutrality that was at the same time denied, one that in addition was made outside the state whose capture was simultaneously being anticipated?

We might argue that secularism remains a polemical category because it is deployed in order to capture the state while never fully inhabiting it. For as in colonial times, during which its exclusion from state power made for a nationalism grounded in society and its cultural or religious languages, Indian politics today continues to be divided between state and society. This is nowhere more evident than in the way in which even the most powerful of India's governments have never been able or indeed willing to monopolize the use of violence in the classical form, as defined by Max Weber, that is meant to characterize nation states as opposed to feudal, absolutist or imperial ones. On the contrary, they tolerate and even rely upon what we might describe as 'social' violence, whether or not it is encouraged and even organized by agents of the state.

This inability or unwillingness to monopolize the use of violence in its own name, I want to argue, illustrates neither the weakness nor backwardness of the Indian state, but instead constitutes its dynamic structural logic, one that has again come into its own after India's liberalization in the 1990s, when society in the form of the private sector and informal economy re-emerged as important sites of political contestation. In this sense, the non-Weberian character of the Indian state is as linked to neo-liberalism today as it had been, in the colonial past, to the anticipatory politics of a nationalism that based itself in society. And it is the BJP that is now in the position of traversing the path from social to state power, and wrestling as Congress once did with the problem of striking a balance between the two, if one can indeed be found.

Hindu nationalism, which in the form of the RSS (the Rashtriya Swayamsevak Sangh), has repeatedly been banned, and thus deprived of a political life in public institutions, has for a long time now represented the quintessential form that social power takes in India. For by the time Indira Gandhi's premiership came to an end, the once formidable social base of the Congress had been whittled away as the party chose to concentrate its power in the institutions of the state. Of course, it continued to rely upon non-state actors, most violently during the anti-Sikh pogroms of 1984 following Mrs Gandhi's assassination by her Sikh bodyguards. But these did not represent the kind of mass base that the Congress had possessed in colonial times. Hindu nationalism, on the other hand, augmented its social power while keeping it separate from the fortunes of the BJP as a political party, though this relationship has been placed under strain whenever the latter has been in government.

More interesting than the shifting balance of power between the BJP and its 'family' of non-state Hindu organizations, however, might be the fact that Hindu nationalism has never possessed a theory of state. Unlike the vision of an Islamic state, for instance, with its distinctive if non-egalitarian constitutional structure, Hindu nationalism has no alternative political model, apart from an insistence on the dominance of majoritarian culture and concerns. And this is its triumph as much as tragedy, since the absence of a distinctive theory of state repeatedly casts Hindu nationalism back into a social movement, one that can only make claims on cultural and demographic rather than constitutional grounds. And in this sense it is the most appropriate heir of a concept of secularism that had always been populist in its argumentation. If anyone has recognized this, it is, unsurprisingly, the Muslim 'fundamentalists' who support secularism in India, but want an Islamic state where they are in a majority. They deny the hypocrisy of this position by arguing that since Hindu nationalism has no theory of state, and so no critique of secularism, it might be oppressive but is still capable of being secular.

But the fact that Hindu nationalism possesses no theory of state also means that it carries the non-Weberian logic of Indian politics to its conclusion, by refusing to depoliticize social life or condemn its concerns as 'irrational' and 'superstitious'. In doing so it is not only heir to the whole history of nationalism in colonial India, but at the same time is also best placed to capitalize on the importance of 'civil society' activism in our own neo-liberal times. Commentary on both secularism and communalism in India has tended to focus too readily on plots and conspiracies that are meant to illustrate the coming together of sinister caste, class and other interests with popular prejudice and fear. But while accurate in some ways, these modes of understanding may be too superficial in others. We should attend instead to the structural and historical factors that define Indian politics, which appear to show a much greater continuity between parties and politics than is usually recognized to be the case.

COALITION KARMA

In light of such continuities, how might we see the changes brought in by the BJP's victory in the 2014 general elections? Having initiated the era of coalition governments in 1999, the BJP brought it to a close, after fifteen tumultuous years, in 2014. The two great coalitions that governed India during this period were known for financial corruption and political paralysis, which go hand in hand with the horse-trading characteristic of such governments. But on occasion they also delivered strong economic growth, while at the same time demonstrating the remarkable resilience of the Indian republic. For to make these enormous coalitions work was an achievement unimagined in the history and practice of democracy. What, then, does their demise tell us about India's political future?

While they are often seen as manifestations of political weakness, coalition governments in India emerged from the deepening reality of federalism through the effective devolution of wealth and power to regional states and even local authorities. The fact that Modi became prime minister without holding any national position in his party is surely a demonstration of this, since never before has the chief minister (he was chief minister of Gujarat) of a particular state managed to achieve power at the Centre. But the coalitions which his election have put to an end also harked back to an older political form, one exemplified by Congress in the days before Indira Gandhi turned it into a top-down command structure. The big-tent approach, which had in some part characterized the Congress since colonial times, made for a politics that was pragmatic and ideological at the same time, reducing nationality to an uneasy conglomeration of disparate interests, even as it subordinated these to a certain vision of India's future. The first and certainly most distinctive example of such a process was represented by the way in which Gandhi's politics of non-violence was paired with Congress deal making.

Unlike communist or fascist parties elsewhere, the different constituencies with which Congress struck such deals continued to maintain their distinctiveness, albeit within a hierarchical structure, and in no case were they crushed or eliminated altogether. It is easy to see why an anti-colonial movement without state power might best be represented by a conglomerate of interests, as well as why such a form should be inappropriate for an independent country where democracy requires a multiplicity of parties representing different interests. And, indeed, even in colonial times the Congress was unable to represent the nation as a whole, opposed as it was by ostensibly more 'modern' parties like the Muslim League, the Republican Party, the Communist Party of India and others that claimed to represent particular interests. It is almost as though these other parties had attempted to institute the integuments of a multiparty democracy in the country even before she had become independent.

One of the perils of Congress's 'inclusive' politics of deal making between differing constituencies, of which the coalition era that has just passed provided only an externalized example, was its 'pragmatic' reduction to pure instrumentality. Such pragmatism can make for violence as much as compromise, and it is this kind of reductive politics that, with the faltering of a strongly ideological element, all Indian parties seem to have inherited from the colonial past. Yet by putting an end to coalition governments, Modi has not returned to Mrs Gandhi's model of party rule, not least because his victory has divided provincial from national politics, rather than replacing one by the other. Far from destroying the 'identity politics' of caste, language or religion, these elections appear to have reserved them for increasingly important regional arenas, while making for a newly constituted and far more limited national one in which the much-invoked 'idea of India' might be rediscovered by those who wish to do so. This seems to have been the great correction effected through the ballot box in 2014.

The demise of coalition government, however, goes beyond the external relations of India's parties to affect their internal structures as well. Over the past fifteen years, after all, neither the Congress nor the BJP was defined by a hierarchical command structure, each being described instead by shifting arrangements of power. With the former it was the relationship between the party's president and prime minister that was crucial, and with the latter that between the party and other members of the Sangh Parivar, the extended Hindu nationalist family. Modi's triumph has destroyed both these forms of constantly negotiated authority. Theoretically, he is no longer beholden to the Sangh, just as the Congress may no longer be sworn to uphold the Nehru–Gandhi family, though in neither case can these dependencies be entirely written off.

Their sometimes anxious collegiality apart, these internal arrangements of power had possessed a mixed blessing for both the Congress and the BJP, that of being able to outsource violence. Like others in the region, successive Indian governments have relied upon extra-state forces to do their dirty work, through caste, religious and other groups, though such operations are largely confined to border problems and marginal populations. While making for plausible deniability, such outsourcing at the same time prevented the creation of a large-scale police state, of which we only caught a glimpse during the Emergency. (Mrs Gandhi imposed an internal Emergency in June

1975 to circumvent calls for her resignation after her election to the Lok Sabha was declared null and void by courts for alleged electoral malpractices.) The rationalization of political structures in the new dispensation, then, may disallow such outsourced violence, but at the same time make the state more responsible for it. This is its promise and its risk.

In some ways the BJP's victory was as much a product of the party's weakness as its strength. What was remarkable about Modi's much commented-upon destruction of its national leadership in order to come to power was the fact that he was able to do so with such apparent ease. After two successive defeats, the BJP had been weakened internally and was desperate to be in government again, thus making for the kind of messianic expectation that allowed another 'outsider', Barack Obama, to take leadership of the Democratic Party, and with it the presidency of the United States. While the two men might not otherwise be comparable, the fervent and faith-based mobilization that brought them both to power is strikingly similar, and suggests that political developments in India follow a global as much as domestic script.

Curiously, the task facing the BJP is the same as that confronting Congress: to rebuild a party that has been destroyed by victory in one case and defeat in the other. Only such a rebuilding will allow either to resist the temptation of populism on the one hand and caste or religious polarization on the other, to say nothing about that represented by the influence of corporate capital. These are the forms of temptation to which Indian parties have routinely submitted, and they indicate political weakness not strength. Will Modi use his popular mandate to build a party that is capable of surviving the force of his own personality? If India's new prime minister means to institutionalize the new arena of national politics that has opened up before him, he is bound to do so.

GOVERNANCE VS GOVERNMENT

The political debate in India has been dominated over the past few years by just two issues: security and corruption. Both are marked by their malleability, with concerns about security shifting from terrorism to rape, and those about corruption moving easily between the criticism of individuals and institutions. Such issues are no longer in the control of political parties or the state, and are as likely to be used by them as against. For whether it is a single man, or the entire government that is blamed for threats to security and the impunity of corruption, these problems are now posed as those of governance. And the language of governance is dominated by the desire for equality as an undifferentiated and so universal good, rather than, say, justice as one that is based on discriminating between citizens.

The social movements that increasingly tend to give these undifferentiated issues their visibility often share their activists and forms of expression with one another. Candlelight vigils, for example, emerged in the 1990s to publicize the murder of young women like Jessica Lall and Priyadarshini Mattoo, whose assailants could evade justice because of their political connections. In the following decade such practices were extended to commemorate terrorist attacks, and today protests against both rape and corruption switch between silent vigils and angry demonstrations as modes of expression. These largely middle-class manifestations of discontent are also unprecedented, given the fact that political parties are still largely absent in their organization.

Such novel forms of mobilization date from the period of India's economic liberalization which created a new space for organization and debate in an increasingly mediatized civil society. But while they have dominated popular interest nationally, what goes unnoticed is how these debates still have little traction for regional politics where the inequalities of caste, class and community continue to define both protest and voting patterns. There seems to be a widening gulf between politics at the state level, whose influence has been expanded by the steady devolution of power in the country, and at the Centre which I have argued is increasingly and for the first time clearly 'national' in its concerns and policies.

The achievement of a 'national' government in 2014 after more than a decade, therefore, followed up and even fulfilled the 'civil society' mobilizations over security and corruption that had preceded it, and that were so concerned with recovering the nation as an undifferentiated, even anti-political idea. Such mobilizations are led by social movements that are highly critical of party politics, setting governance against government in forms like the anti-corruption Jan Lokpal Bill, which sought to make Parliament accountable to civil society beyond the electoral process. After all, issues like corruption or security are so unexceptionable as to be universal, and define the nation outside politics by excluding any substantive opposition.

While both social movements and the political parties that seek their support proclaim their allegiance to the country's founding fathers, the governance that preoccupies them does not belong to a national history. If anything, it was the colonial state that sought to justify itself by the language of fair and competent administration. Since it was run by foreigners who did not depend on elections or 'vote banks', the administration was, by definition, thought to be impartial and non-political. And by the end of colonial rule the vocabulary of 'development' had come to lend additional legitimacy to an unaccountable bureaucracy, from where it has been inherited by equally unrepresentative international organizations and 'global civil society'.

But as a global category, governance achieved its current status during the 'post-ideological' period following the cold war. Premised on the retrenchment of the state, which was meant to outsource many of its former functions to private enterprises, NGOs and other institutions of civil society, governance redefined government as managerial oversight. In the form of 'good governance', management was promoted by international organizations like the UN, NATO, World Bank and the

IMF, at least initially to manage the transition of post-Soviet societies to democracy and capitalism.

Governance of this kind was explicitly anti-political, and meant to reduce the hold of a corrupt and tyrannical state upon its citizens. Yet, the social movements that emerged to oppose such states have been able in spectacular cases like the 'colour' revolutions of eastern Europe or those of the Arab Spring more recently to topple governments but not to form them. Given their distaste for party politics, it could not have been otherwise. So, while it is remarkable that the Gandhian social activist Anna Hazare's 'India Against Corruption' movement spawned the Aam Aadmi Party (AAP), its inability to balance a social movement with institutional politics, or transform one into the other, is unsurprising.

A precedent for this may be found in Hindu nationalism, India's first great social movement of the post-cold-war period. Achieving a massive mobilization in the media-saturated civil society created by liberalization, Hindu nationalism is propagated by a political party, the BJP, and apparently non-political organizations such as the RSS, the VHP and the Bajrang Dal, which together constitute the hybrid association of the Sangh Parivar. Rather than merely conspiratorial, the secretive character of the RSS, for instance, serves to demonstrate its deliberate policy of working outside an arena defined by the institutions of parliamentary democracy, while still being part of a 'family' that includes a political party.

Perhaps because the Sangh Parivar appears to have been shut out of party politics in a way that the BJP couldn't do under the leadership of Atal Bihari Vajpayee, elements within it seem to have taken their quest for power and influence back to the civil society which has always been their home turf since the days when the RSS was banned from public life. Hence, the proliferating controversies and the potential for violence that goes with them over issues such as hate speech, 'love jihad', disputes over the building of temples and programmes to 'reconvert'

Muslims and Christians. The BJP has struggled, with varying degrees of purpose and success, to free itself from Hindu nationalism as a social movement, or rather to subordinate the latter to parliamentary politics. Will its vision of becoming normalized as India's conservative party be fulfilled at the hands of a leader who, ironically, is the man most associated with Hindu nationalism as a social movement?

HINDU NATIONALISM AND THE REPUBLIC

Will the BJP, finally, manage to absorb the social movement that gave rise to it, or will the latter's attempt to recover the nation in non-political terms end up establishing a majority-defined democracy against the republic? Being a political category, the republic is opposed to majority rule as a social form, meant as it is to create a public space in which majorities and minorities are made up of shifting and temporary interests, rather than the permanent demographic facts that populism on the Left as much as the Right relies upon. This was, in fact, the chief concern of Muhammad Ali Jinnah (the Muslim League leader and founder of Pakistan) in opposing Congress. For he believed that it was because Muslims in colonial India were too numerous to constitute a minority, forming as they did regional majorities in sizeable parts of the country, that these religious categories had become so intractable politically.

Yet, Jinnah's solution, to break up the country and make Muslims and Hindus into real and therefore politically irrelevant majorities and minorities in its successor states, proved not to be a workable one in either. For there exist parties in both countries that seek to make permanent political majorities of each religion. Perhaps it is because these religious groups have never been able to constitute such majorities, either in India or Pakistan, that the anxiety to fix them into place politically continues to be so high within both. In a sense, the attempt to 'normalize' Hindu nationalism politically by presenting it as a cultural form with which all religious groups can and should identify, however unequally, can be seen as another way of rendering religion itself irrelevant in political life – and producing a new kind of national culture that might serve as a unifying backdrop to the immense diversity of Indian causes and identities. Indeed, it is this effort that might weld Hindu nationalism and governance into the same project.

However disingenuous such a claim might appear, it does possess a clearly nationalist logic, one familiar enough from the history of the European nation state. And it is this logic that requires the existence of a social movement for its fulfilment. The only parties that depend upon social movements in India today, both in the service of this logic, are the gigantic BJP on the one hand, and fledgling AAP on the other. Although they are very different and in fact opposed to each other, it is instructive that both parties stake their reputations on governance rather than government. Does the devolution of power in India, and its consequent political fragmentation, suggest that the Centre can only hold in such non-statist ways, by producing a national culture? Is the national arena demarcated by the media fated to represent civil society with the state serving as its agent in ensuring good governance under the watchful eye of a Lokpal or Vikas Purush (Development Man)? Only those who still act in the world of politics can answer these questions.

View from Pakistan: 'Religious' Politics and the Democratic Political Process

Beena Sarwar

~ψ~

Beena Sarwar is a writer, documentary film-maker and artist who has been engaged as a journalist and activist in human rights and peace issues for over two decades, most recently as an editor for Aman ki Asha, a peace initiative between India and Pakistan.

The political rise and election of Narendra Modi as prime minister of India aroused anxiety in India as well as in Pakistan. Many Indians feared an onslaught on the secular values enshrined in India's Constitution. Pakistanis were wary, given Modi's anti-Pakistan, anti-Muslim history.

But while Modi may symbolize divisive forces in India, as prime minister he must deliver on the development agenda for which he was elected, and distance himself from the 'saffron brigade'. In the long run, the deep-rooted democracy in India, for all its aberrations and weaknesses, is likely to eventually neutralize sectarian elements and prevent them from imposing their agenda.

Communal forces in both India and Pakistan broadly mirror each other. Extremists on both sides equate religion with patriotism and are quick to accuse others of being traitors or anti-religion. As much as there are lessons for Pakistan in India's democratic political process (barring Indira Gandhi's Emergency rule, 1975–77), India can also learn from Pakistan's experience, where injecting religion into politics has led to disastrous consequences.

Some Indians object to any comparison with Pakistan, arguing that India is in a different league, an economic power to reckon with, while Pakistan remains mired in the past, racked by violence stemming from its own policies. This is an oversimplification of a complex situation.

For one thing, although Pakistan has never elected extremist or communal parties to power, these elements have gained ground over the years due to various factors, including Pakistan's geopolitically strategic location. This has led to Pakistan becoming a proxy battleground for international players like America, Saudi Arabia, Iran and more lately China. Since the Afghan war in the 1980s, extremists in Pakistan operating in the name of religion have been immeasurably strengthened. These retrogressive forces reject democracy. They don't represent the people but due to bully tactics and street power, they unduly influence politics. The emergence of a democratic polity in Pakistan now threatens their power.

The continuation of a democratic political process in the long term neutralizes communalism and militancy. Today, the world faces violent extremism in various forms along with economic and social inequalities and unequal political power structures. Problems persist even in advanced countries – for example, racially motivated murders and school shootings in the United States, Nazi revivalists and white supremacists in Europe and England. Leaving aside the correlation between inequalities and militancy, criminal-minded hardliners operating in the name of religion clearly pose stronger challenges in less developed countries mired in tradition like India and Pakistan that already face tensions due to rampant disparities and unplanned urbanization.

The words of Pakistan's founding father Muhammad Ali Jinnah in his first address as president of the Constituent Assembly of Pakistan on 11 August 1947 should have set the tone for the new country. Jinnah asserted that after the 'unavoidable' Partition of India, each citizen, from any community, colour, caste or creed, 'is first, second and last a citizen of this State with equal rights, privileges and obligations.'

Working in that spirit, he said, would eventually erase all divisions between not only Hindus and Muslims but also within communities, 'because even as regards the Muslims, you have Pathans, Punjabis, Shias, Sunnis and so on. Among the Hindus you have Brahmans, Vaishnavites, Khatries, also Bengalis, Madrasis.' These divisions had been 'the biggest hindrance in the way of India to attain its freedom and independence'.

All citizens of Pakistan were free, proclaimed Jinnah. 'You are free to go to your temples. You are free to go to your mosques or any other place of worship in this State of Pakistan. You may belong to any religion or caste or creed. That has nothing to do with the business of the State ... I think you should keep that in front of us as our ideal, and you will find that in the course of time Hindus will cease to be Hindus and Muslims will cease to be Muslims, not in the religious sense because that is the personal faith of each individual, but in the political sense, as citizens of the State.'

This was an assertion of pluralism in the new country. It was also a vague manifesto, perhaps deliberately so according to Jinnah's biographer Hector Bolitho, given the difficulties of developing a secular system in a country founded in the name of religion.

Jinnah enunciated his conviction on several occasions that Pakistan would not be a theocracy. But bringing religion into politics has its own dynamics.

EERIE PARALLELS

Extremists in India and Pakistan are essentially two sides of the same coin. They feed on each other with their anti-Pakistan and anti-India rhetoric respectively. Communal forces in India glorify the murderer of Mahatma Gandhi as a hero. Their counterparts in Pakistan glorify Mumtaz Qadri who assassinated the Punjab governor Salmaan Taseer. Caste-based violence is all too common in India, just as it is in Pakistan – where it is often disguised as 'religious' violence as in the case of Aasia Bibi, the Christian woman convicted and sentenced to death after being charged with 'blasphemy'.

India and Pakistan also have in common contradictions arising from the pace of social change juxtaposed with traditional, conservative values, particularly with regard to caste and gender. The 'India shining' slogan notwithstanding, the fault lines there bear an eerie resemblance to the situation in Pakistan. Mutual problems include economic inequality, gender violence, 'honour' killings, widespread illiteracy and child labour, and unplanned urbanization. Additionally, there is often impunity for those with connections in the circles of power. This gives an opening for criminals to operate and for communal forces to polarize society. In India, extremists are pushing an agenda of Hindu supremacy with attempts like the 'ghar wapsi' drive to 'reconvert' Muslims and Christians, rewriting textbooks, imposing Hindu nationalism, and attacking Indians who celebrate non-Indian festivals like Valentine's Day.

In Pakistan, extremists kidnap Hindu girls and get them married to Muslims as part of a deliberate strategy to make inroads into Sindh, the province with the largest Hindu population in Pakistan. The situation is exacerbated by the influx of money, religious seminaries, and radical preachers from the Gulf states, particularly Saudi Arabia. In this situation, Pakistanis like advocates Asma Jahangir, Amarnath Motumal and their colleagues at the non-government Human Rights Commission of Pakistan (HRCP) are like a David pitted against a Goliath. David may well win in the end in Pakistan. But it will take time. In the meantime, innocent Pakistanis will continue to pay a huge price.

The common problems India and Pakistan face include gender violence and the killing of hundreds of women every year on the pretext of 'honour'. Traditionally, 'honour'-based violence is contained within a family or community, with the perpetrators punishing their 'own' women for alleged transgressions. However, in Pakistan, 'Islamic' militants like the Taliban and their affiliated groups have crossed these barriers and freely threaten and attack women of other communities.

Recognizing the commonalities, ordinary people, artists, writers, activists and intellectuals in Pakistan have long stressed the need to build bridges with India. Key stakeholders, from major political parties to the business community, now also support the political consensus for peace with India that has developed in Pakistan over recent years.

However, a fringe element still clings to the outdated pro-'jihad', anti-India narrative perpetuated by sections of the security establishment and the 'religious' groups the army once nurtured in order to gain 'strategic depth' in Afghanistan and an upper hand over India, particularly over Kashmir. I use the word 'religious' in quotes when referring to the politics of the 'religious parties' in India and Pakistan, because religion is the pretext these parties use to gain power. This lobby equates being a patriotic Pakistani with being Muslim and anti-India – although India's Muslim population exceeds Pakistan's total population.

One of the spokespersons of this anti-India lobby is Hafiz Saeed who heads the banned 'religious' charity Jama'at-ud-Dawa (JUD), another incarnation of the infamous Lashkar-e-Tayyaba (LeT) that is involved with militancy in Kashmir. Washington has head money on Saeed for his links to the Mumbai attacks of November 2008, but the JUD openly holds rallies in major cities and keeps the anti-India narrative alive in Pakistan.

Groups like JUD/LeT in Pakistan have gained ground due to policies formulated not by elected governments but by the security establishment. The political vacuum created by military rule and the injection of religion into politics has strengthened militancy in Pakistan. There is genuine apprehension about the rise of extremism in India where the 2002 pogrom against Muslims in Gujarat took place under Modi's watch as chief minister. More than a decade later, he owes his election as prime minister to his development, rather than communal, agenda.

GUJARAT AND MUMBAI

Modi has never been convicted of the crimes against humanity of which he is accused. Neither has Hafiz Saeed. One was allegedly involved in a pogrom against a religious minority community in the state he headed as a political representative. The other, who has never been elected, is allegedly behind the massacres of members of a religious community (Shia Muslims) in Pakistan, and attacks on Indian soil. In both cases, courts have so far acquitted them for lack of evidence.

Indians who ask why the Pakistan courts acquit people like Hafiz Saeed forget that our court systems are basically the same. Both countries inherited the same set of British-era colonial laws in 1947. But while India under Jawaharlal Nehru got to work on a Constitution and land reforms, Pakistan retained its Provisional (Interim) Constitution, adapted from the Government of India Act of 1935, with various amendments and alterations for almost a decade after Independence.

Obtaining convictions is not easy. Pakistan has no witness protection programme. This, coupled with poor forensics and prosecution techniques, and controversial laws imposed by a military dictator in the name of religion, has created a culture of impunity and allows criminals to literally get away with murder. Any litigation involves a long and cumbersome process with several levels of appeal. When on 26 December 2014 a district court in Pakistan announced that it was granting bail to Zaki ur Rehman Lakhvi, accused of the November 2008 Mumbai attacks, the Pakistan government contested the court order (at the time of writing in February 2015, Lakhvi was still in prison; he obtained bail in April). There was a furious reaction in India where there seemed to be an expectation that Pakistan would bypass due process when it came to militants.

For decades Pakistan has seen the military guard not just the country's physical frontiers but also take upon itself the task of guarding its ideological frontiers, projected as being synonymous with Islam. This has much to do with the political vacuum caused by the subversion of democratic political process.

Some Pakistanis express nostalgia for the days of military rule when law and order and the economy were under control. Some Indians also look nostalgically at General Pervez Musharraf's stint in power as a kind of golden era between Pakistan and India. Yet, as Pakistan's army chief, Musharraf was the architect of the 1999 Kargil war that brought the two nations to the brink of a nuclear war. He is on record saying that he is 'proud' of the Kargil operation that he masterminded 'in revenge' against India's role in the division of Pakistan and creation of Bangladesh in 1971. A few months after the Kargil war, Musharraf usurped power in a military coup, and headed an illegitimate regime for nearly a decade.

Musharraf also played a duplicitous game post-9/11 as he ran with the hares and hunted with the hounds. Under Musharraf, Pakistan was the last government to cut off diplomatic ties with the 'bad Taliban' in Afghanistan, and that too when pushed by Washington. But Musharraf allowed Pakistan's home-grown militants to function, like the 'good Taliban' and their affiliates – those who supposedly further Pakistan's foreign policy objectives of bleeding India and 'strategic depth' in Afghanistan.

India and Pakistan did come close to a rapprochement under Musharraf. But a one-man band doesn't need political consensus to take decisions. His 'boys' unquestioningly obeyed his orders because that's what soldiers do. Not so the 'bloody civilians'. Democracy is a messy business. Elected representatives have to answer to a constituency – and in Pakistan, also to the security establishment. An elected head of government must obtain parliamentary consent for policy decisions.

Military rule, on the other hand, keeps things under control artificially, including prices. It's like a pressure cooker from which the steam isn't allowed to escape. When the lid is lifted, whatever is stewing in the pot erupts.

In India, the existence of a democratic political process enables a continuous letting off of the steam, preventing its contents from erupting. This eventually neutralizes the potential dangers when communally minded politicians are elected into power. With the eyes of the world and the Indian electorate upon him, Modi has to distance himself from right-wing extremists causing havoc in the name of religion. He may not condemn them or take strong action but he cannot afford to let them run totally amok.

In Pakistan, on the other hand, extremist forces have been immensely strengthened by religion-based politics perpetuated by Zia ul Haq during his decade-long (1978–88) military regime. The so-called Islamic laws imposed during that time, coupled with the indoctrination, training and arms provided to the 'mujahideen' during the Afghan war contributed to a veritable army of indoctrinated militants who now want to occupy power and impose their version of Islam on the entire state. Since the Afghan war, the extremists have mutated into multiple splinter groups who, despite their differences, are ideologically aligned against democracy, democratic values, human rights, women's rights and cultural freedoms.

If this has echoes of India's saffron brigade, that's because they are, as mentioned earlier, mirror images of each other. The difference is that in Pakistan, extremists are trying to impose their agenda through armed militancy, while in India, 'religious' extremists are trying to do this through the political system. There is a glimmer of hope in Pakistan having taken the first steps on the path to a democratic, political process, with an elected government having completed its tenure and handed over power to the next elected government for the first time although this happened as late as in 2013.

Only when the democratic political process is allowed to continue, do citizens have a platform to voice their views. After the horrific attacks on Mumbai in November 2008, attempts by Modi and his Bharatiya Janata Party (BJP) to communalize the issue with anti-Pakistan and anti-Muslim sentiments did not yield them victory in the state elections held shortly afterwards. When the Modi government at the Centre failed to deliver on its development agenda, the electorate rejected the BJP in the Delhi state elections in 2015, despite a high-octave campaign and attempts to polarize the electorate. Arvind Kejriwal's Aam Admi Party (AAP) swept the polls – a reminder, if one is needed, of the power of the electorate.

COMMUNAL POLITICS

India's voter turnout in the 2014 general elections was nearly 67 per cent, out of which Modi's BJP polled 31 per cent, that is, barely 21 per cent, less than a quarter of the total eligible voters, or about a fifth of the total electorate. The remaining four-fifths did not vote for Modi/BJP, and a large part of the fifth that did was the negative vote against the incumbents rather than a positive vote for Modi/BJP. But even narrow margins win seats in a parliamentary democracy. At a glance, it may look like a 'saffron wave', but the electorate has made clear their distaste for communal politics.

In Pakistan too the electorate has consistently voted for parties that are not communal. There was massive bloodshed in the run-up to the May 2013 elections and fears of violence on polling day itself. The Taliban had denounced the process as 'un-Islamic' and attacked electoral candidates and rallies, killing over a 100 people in the previous month. Yet Pakistan saw its highest-ever voter turnout, 55 per cent. People came out in unprecedentedly large numbers to vote, as much for political parties as against the Taliban. There had been opinion polls about Pakistanis' growing sympathies for 'religious' parties. However, when it came to the real and the biggest opinion poll – the general elections – the people of Pakistan made their views clear: they gave a resounding 'no' to Talibanization.

Extremists operating in the name of religion in Pakistan have gained strength as a result of policies not democratically formulated but imposed by the security establishment. Post-9/11, after Pakistan began changing that policy, the extremists turned their guns on state symbols like police academies, intelligence offices and military bases. Attacks such as on the Peshawar Army Public School on 16 December 2014 show the increasing desperation of the militants at losing the war.

Until then, Pakistan marked 16 December every year as a 'black day' to mark the surrender of the Pakistan Army to India in Dhaka in 1971. In 2014, the significance of this day was overshadowed by the massacre in Peshawar that drew an unprecedented response from around the world, especially India. The hashtag #IndiaWithPakistan began trending spontaneously on social media within hours of the attack, with over 63,000 tweets on Tuesday, the day of the tragedy. By Friday, the number of tweets tagged #IndiaWithPakistan had crossed the one million mark. In another poignant gesture, Modi appealed for a two-minute silence at schools across India.

INDIA–PAKISTAN RELATIONS

Despite Modi's heart-warming gesture and despite the goodwill that clearly exists between the people of both countries, India–Pakistan relations have worsened under Modi. An increasingly restrictive visa policy makes it difficult even for members of divided families to meet. India's intransigence on this front seems to have increased since the Modi government was elected. India denied visas to twenty-four prominent Pakistanis invited to a seminar in Delhi on 'Understanding Pakistan', organized by the Pakistan–India People's Forum for Peace and Democracy (PIPFPD) during 19–21 December 2014 (the visas were granted later, delaying the seminar till March 2015). Formed in 1994, PIPFPD is the oldest and largest people-to-people group between India and Pakistan. Both governments have in the past granted visas for PIPFPD conventions to citizens of the other country, leaving a door open even during hostilities.

The growth of the Internet and social media have allowed Indians and Pakistanis to surmount the visa difficulties and connect through platforms like Aman ki Asha (a platform for peace jointly launched by Pakistan's Jang group of newspapers and *The Times of India*), the peace video selfies ('velfies') of the 'Dear Neighbour Movement', the Indo-Pak Peace Calendar launched by the cross-border youth organization Aaghaz-e-Dosti and countless other such initiatives.

However, both sides continue to violate the 2003 ceasefire along the disputed border that divides Kashmir. Each blames the other for 'unprovoked' firing that kills civilians and soldiers on both sides. Security establishments on either side provide whatever little information appears in the public domain about what is happening at the border. Very few journalists question the official narratives or have the access to produce more in-depth, nuanced reports. Both sides typically report only their own casualties. This provides a greater space to warmongering extremists, hawks and fanatics. Political leaders fall into sabre-rattling rhetoric with sound bites like 'munh-tor jawab' (jaw-breaking responses) and 'boli nahin goli' (bullets not talks).

The overwhelming and genuine response in India to the Peshawar school massacre was a strong counter to the anti-India narrative peddled by Pakistan's security establishment that has been making major policy decisions for too long. Given the power of this security establishment, it is understandable for Indians to ask why they should bother talking to an elected government in Pakistan at all. But, in the long run, only an elected government can legitimately make policy changes. There are no short cuts. The Taliban and their affiliated groups have made great inroads in Pakistan, enabled by the 'good Taliban, bad Taliban' policy. A mess that has taken over sixty years to make cannot be fixed overnight. In the long run, the biggest blow to the extremist militants would be for democracy in Pakistan to take root and continue, and for India and Pakistan to unite against them.

Pakistan's political timeline (see Appendix) shows how democracy has been subverted and prevented from taking root in the country. In contrast, India's continuing democratic political process demonstrates how it is able to check extremist forces from gaining the upper hand. As India faces the rise of Hindutva forces, it must learn from the Pakistani experience the danger of inserting religion into politics, particularly when religion is conflated with national identity.

In India, extremists in the name of Hinduism are trying to push the narrative that to be a true Indian you also have to be a Hindu. They label as traitors those who resist this concept. Similarly, in Pakistan, hyper-nationalists term as 'traitors' and 'infidels' those who question or oppose the 'two-nation theory'.

There are greater dangers associated with such demonization in Pakistan than in India. Armed, trained men indoctrinated with Takfiri ideology (Muslims declaring other Muslims to be 'kafir' or non-believer) target Shia and Ahmadi communities in Pakistan. They also carry out attacks inspired – even trained – by Takfiri militants like

Daish, Al Qaeda or Taliban. As Hillary Clinton famously said, 'You can't keep snakes in your backyard and expect them only to bite your neighbours. Eventually those snakes are going to turn on whoever has them in the backyard.'

The bottom line is that criminal acts must be dealt with as such. The rule of law must be applied and due process followed, regardless of the perpetrator's religion or motivation, whether it is religion, nationalism or honour.

We are starting to see evidence of this in India where at least some perpetrators of the 2002 carnage in Gujarat have been convicted and sentenced, belatedly and insufficiently perhaps, but it is a start. The painful process continues. Few perpetrators of earlier mass crimes like the 1984 massacre of Sikhs following Indira Gandhi's assassination have been brought to book. But going forward, given increased awareness, tools and platforms that enhance the voice of the people, it will be increasingly difficult for such pogroms to take place.

In the coming years, India must decide in which direction it wants to go. Indians who criticize the shrill nationalist religious narrative in Pakistan must look inward and contemplate the damage that a similar voice within their own country is causing. This is something Prime Minister Modi and others will have to consider in the long term if they want to achieve continued electoral success in India.

APPENDIX

PAKISTAN AND THE DEMOCRATIC POLITICAL PROCESS: A POLITICAL TIMELINE

1947–58: The first war between India and Pakistan over Kashmir in 1948. Pakistan's founding father Muhammed Ali Jinnah dies in September 1948. Jinnah's successor Liaquat Ali Khan is assassinated in 1951. Pakistan's first Constitution, adopted in 1956, proclaims Pakistan to be an Islamic republic. In 1958, President Iskander Mirza declares the country's first martial law. Two weeks later Field Marshal Ayub Khan deposes him.

1958–71: Ayub Khan proclaims himself president in 1960. In 1965, Pakistan fights its second war with India over Kashmir. Gen. Yahya Khan takes over in 1969 after Ayub Khan resigns. Pakistan holds elections in 1970. The Awami League wins, but isn't allowed to take over power.

1971–77: Pakistan breaks up in 1971 following the West Pakistan establishment's refusal to allow the winning Awami League of then East Pakistan to form government. The subsequent military onslaught on East Pakistan and the ensuing civil war ends with Pakistan's humiliating surrender to India on 16 December 1971 and the emergence of Bangladesh as an independent nation. Instead of putting paid to the 'two-nation theory' according to which Hindus and Muslims form two separate nations, the self-proclaimed keepers of the 'ideology of Pakistan' continue to propagate it.

The country's first elected prime minister, Zulfiqar Ali Bhutto, comes to power on the back of the army, with army chief Gen. Yahya Khan resigning and handing over the government to him after secession of Bangladesh. (In the years since, despite many setbacks and problems, Bangladesh has made great strides in areas like education and the separation of state from religion. Meanwhile, Pakistan continues to reel under a situation that has spiralled almost out of control, fuelled by a 'Takfiri' ideology.)

Pakistan's Parliament under Bhutto finally passes a Constitution on 10 April 1973. On 7 September 1974, the National Assembly passes the second constitutional amendment, declaring Ahmadis as a non-Muslim minority. Appeasing the 'religious' right will not save Bhutto.

1977–88: In July 1977, army chief Gen. Zia ul Haq overthrows the Pakistan People's Party (PPP) government, and gets Bhutto hanged in 1979 on trumped-up murder charges.

The Zia regime makes various changes to the Constitution in the name of Islam, immeasurably strengthening the 'religious' right. These measures have furthered a narrative that supports 'religious' militancy. Militant groups have claimed the lives of over 50,000 civilian and over 10,000 armed forces personnel over the last decade.

1988–99: Zia is killed in a mid-air explosion in August 1988. Pakistan undergoes a period of what I term 'democracy musical chairs'. General elections held in November 1988 bring Benazir Bhutto to power, but the military establishment, used to making policy decisions by now, prevents her from taking oath as prime minister until she agrees to allow them control of three key policy areas – defence, economy and foreign affairs.

But even the crippled government is not allowed to complete its tenure and is dissolved less than two years later under Article 58-2 (b), a Ziaist constitutional amendment imposed in 1985 that allows the president to dismiss an elected government. Article 58-2 (b) is used to dismiss the next two elected governments before completion of their terms – Nawaz Sharif's, and then again Benazir Bhutto's. (After the 2008 elections and restoration of the democratic process, the Pakistan Assembly finally did away with Article 58-2(b), in April 2010.)

Re-elected in 1996, Nawaz Sharif is again overthrown by his army chief Gen. Pervez Musharraf in what journalists like to call a 'bloodless' military coup (all coups in Pakistan have been bloodless) in October 1999.

1999–2008: Musharraf, the last military dictator to rule Pakistan, holds controlled elections in 2002. In the political vacuum created by the exile of leaders like Sharif and Bhutto, the 'religious' parties are able for the first time to form government in one province of Pakistan (North-West Frontier Province, later renamed Khyber Pakhtunkhwa).

Growing political pressure forces Musharraf to allow Bhutto and Sharif to return to Pakistan and participate in the elections of 2008.

After Bhutto is assassinated during an election campaign in December 2007, the Pakistan People's Party is elected to power. Musharraf serves out his term as president until August 2008.

During his regime, Musharraf tries to mend fences with India and even comes close to resolving the Kashmir dispute. The matter ends when his presidential term ends and he is forced to let the elected government appoint the country's next president – a historical transfer of power in Pakistan. But the military establishment continues to call the shots in Pakistan – which may change over time if the democratic political process continues. The process began with the 2008 elections and the peaceful transfer of power following the 2013 elections.

2008–present: The year 2013 marks the first time in Pakistan that an elected government on completion of its tenure handed over power to the next elected government. The democratic political process in this country has barely begun.

REFERENCES

'India With Pakistan hashtag crosses 1 million on Twitter', TNN, 20 December 2014.

Hasan, Arif, *The Unplanned Revolution: Observations on the Process of Socio-Economic Change in Pakistan*, Karachi: City Press, 2002.

Hoodbhoy, Pervez, 'The Menace of Education: What Are They Teaching in Pakistani Schools Today?', *The News on Sunday*, 11 June 2000.

Jalal, Ayesha, *The State of Martial Rule: The Origins of Pakistan's Political Economy of Defence*, Lahore: Sang-e-Meel, 1999.

Jalal, Ayesha, *Jinnah: The Sole Spokesman: Jinnah, the Muslim League and the Demand for Pakistan*, Cambridge University Press, 1985.

Munir, Muhammad, *From Jinnah to Zia*, Lahore: Vanguard, 1980.

Niazi, Zamir, *Press in Chains*, Karachi Press Club (Pakistan), 1986; Ajanta Books (India), 1987.

Sarwar, Beena, 'The Hijacking of Pakistan', *Dispatches from a Wounded World*, December 2001, www.booksurge.com and www.blueear.com

——, 'Role of Women in Building Peace between India and Pakistan: A Pakistani Perspective', in Shree Mulay and Jackie Kirk (eds), *Women Building Peace Between India and Pakistan*, London; New York; Delhi: Anthem Press An Antham Critical Series 2007.

——, 'Media Matters', in Ira Pande (ed.), *The Great Divide: India and Pakistan*, India International Centre, 2010.

——, 'The Other, for us and them', *The Indian Express*, 30 August 2013.

——, 'India-Pakistan: Build on goodwill, not hate', *The News on Sunday*, 11 January 2015.

India under Modi: Will the Turning Point Be Followed by a Point of Return?

Sudheendra Kulkarni

The writer was an aide to former Prime Minister Atal Bihari Vajpayee in the Prime Minister's Office between 1998 and 2004. He was also an activist of the BJP for sixteen years before he quit the party in 2013 due to ideological differences. Comments are welcome at sudheenkulkarni@gmail.com.

The sixteenth of May, 2014, was a turning point in Indian democracy. The Bharatiya Janata Party, with Narendra Modi as its prime ministerial candidate, secured a historic victory in the general elections held that month. After thirty long years, a single party succeeded in winning a clear and decisive mandate on its own: 282 seats in a house of 544. In no election since 1984, when the Congress under the leadership of Rajiv Gandhi and riding a sympathy wave in the wake of Prime Minister Indira Gandhi's assassination, had a single party won a majority in the Lok Sabha. Modi's leadership had helped the BJP attain its highest ever tally, which marked a staggering 100-seat increase from its previous high watermark of 182 seats in 1999.

The result was a turning point in another important respect. The Indian National Congress, India's oldest political party that had ruled for the longest period (forty-nine years) since the country's independence in 1947, suffered its worst-ever electoral defeat. For a party that had secured outright majority in seven previous elections, and had led or supported six coalition governments, the tally was a measly forty-four seats.

By any reckoning, it was a stunning performance by the BJP. Previously, the party, led by its stalwarts Atal Bihari Vajpayee and L.K. Advani, used to claim that its biggest achievement was that it had transformed India's Congress-led unipolar polity into a bipolar one, with the BJP having become the second pole. The claim was justifiable because the BJP, which was founded in 1980, had succeeded in defeating the Congress and forming coalition governments at the Centre after two parliamentary elections, in 1998 and 1999. On both occasions, the governments were led by Vajpayee, the founder as well as the tallest leader of the BJP. For a party that had bitten the dust in the 1984 parliamentary elections, winning only two seats, it was truly an impressive achievement to have become India's ruling party fifteen years later under the leadership of Vajpayee and Advani.

However, Modi demonstrated in 2014 that he could lead the BJP to a victory that far surpassed any that the Vajpayee-Advani duo had achieved. Indeed, in his very first innings as the captain of the BJP, he had succeeded in transforming India's polity into unipolar again. The crucial difference, this time around, was that he had made the BJP the single pole in the country's political establishment. The once-mighty Congress party had not only lost the pole position but had almost been reduced to the level of a regional party – its number of seats in the Lok Sabha was only seven more than that of the All India Anna Dravida

Munnetra Kazhagam (AIADMK), a regional party in Tamil Nadu, whose tally was thirty-seven.

The 2014 election was different for the BJP in another respect. In all previous elections, the party was seen to have been led by a collective leadership. Even though Vajpayee was its undisputed and most charismatic leader, the party functioned under a collegiate structure at the top, with Advani, a highly accomplished leader in his own right, guiding the party organization with the help of old (Kushabhau Thakre, Bhaironsingh Shekhawat, Dr Murli Manohar Joshi, Sundar Singh Bhandari, etc.) and young (Pramod Mahajan, Sushma Swaraj, Arun Jaitley, Narendra Modi, etc.) colleagues. Many of these colleagues had made a mark in public and parliamentary life. The 2014 election changed all that. It was, and also deliberately projected as, Modi's solo show. No other leader really mattered in the BJP. Both before and immediately after the election, Advani had been deliberately and systematically marginalized. Since Vajpayee has remained bedridden for many years – he had anyway become inactive after his government failed to win a renewed mandate in 2004 – the BJP suddenly and irreversibly emerged out of the Atal-Advani era. It entered the Modi era on 16 May 2014.

MODI GOVERNMENT'S FIRST TWENTY MONTHS: A MIX OF POSITIVES AND NEGATIVES

What happens to the BJP under Modi's leadership is really of secondary importance. Of primary importance are the following questions: What happens to India with Modi at the helm of the government? How enduring is the turning point in Indian politics that his victory has effected? Will there be a point of return? And since history does not quite repeat itself in the literal sense of the term, what will be that 'point of return' when the Modi era does come to an end?

An objective and dispassionate examination of these questions after twenty months of Modi's government (at the time of writing this article) shows a mix of positive and negative trends. There are also some troubling signals that the positives could be overshadowed by the negatives if Modi allows himself to be controlled by the Sangh Parivar, the ideology-driven family of the Rashtriya Swayamsevak Sangh (RSS), of which the BJP is a member.

There is no doubt that Modi, as prime minister, has brought considerable innovativeness to bear on the functioning of at least some limbs of the government. For example, the 'Make in India', 'Digital India' and 'Startup India' missions launched by him have the potential to considerably modernize the Indian economy. With India aiming at, and also capable of achieving, a double-digit GDP growth rate, India's manufacturing sector is in urgent need of rapid modernization and expansion so that it becomes one of the main engines of the economy. A country of the size of India has neglected for far too long development of indigenous strengths in defence production, aviation infrastructure, shipbuilding, electronics and IT hardware, heavy and hi-tech engineering, and so on. A crucial infrastructure like railways is in dire need of modernization. The 'Make in India' mission aims at encouraging large-scale domestic and foreign investments into making India a hub of manufacturing to meet internal needs as well as to boost exports. It will also benefit the huge sector of tiny, small and medium enterprises (TSMEs), which provide employment to the bulk of India's workforce.

Similarly, the 'Digital India' mission aims at universalizing the application of digital technologies in all areas of socio-economic development and governance. This can bring enormous benefits in spurring efficiency in the economy, introducing much-needed transparency in governance, and improving education and healthcare. If these two missions are implemented well – and it is still a big 'if' since the bureaucratic machinery Modi has inherited remains change-averse – these also have the potential to create large-scale employment opportunities, which is a pressing need for India's swelling youth population.

Startup India, a mission that seeks to promote innovation-based entrepreneurship, is sure to appeal to young Indians who have bright ideas that can be turned into businesses using new technologies. Israel has shown the spectacular benefits of promoting a 'startup culture'. Its success is also seen in Silicon Valley, where, significantly, a fairly large number of startups are founded by Indians, most of whom are first-generation entrepreneurs. This culture is now rapidly spreading in India. By spotting this trend, and by creating an enabling policy ecosystem to nurture it, Modi has shown that he is looking for new ways of modernizing the Indian economy. Of course, it has to be also noted here that his government has not shown the same alacrity or resolve to make the policy and administrative environment easier for older, traditional or 'already started-up' businesses, which continue to be buffeted by bribery and red-tape.

Modi also deserves to be complimented for launching mass campaigns like the one to popularize Yoga and the other to promote cleanliness ('Swachh Bharat' or Clean India). The latter addresses a deeply entrenched problem that hinders national progress and harms the well-being of our society in so many ways. No other prime minister in the past had given as high a priority to tackling this problem as Modi has. He has also done well to associate this campaign with the name of Mahatma Gandhi because no other leader in modern world history had attached as much importance to cleanliness and sanitation as the Father of the Indian Nation had. Of course, we cannot overlook the fact that the Mahatma had regarded 'Clean Inside' – that is, pure feelings, thoughts and deeds – to be as important as 'Clean Outside'. This Gandhian understanding is not reflected either in the prime minister's utterances on the 'Swachh Bharat' campaign or in the manner in which it is being implemented by his government. The campaign is also encountering many problems on the ground, the chief being the apathy of both the populace and the government machinery. Nevertheless, Modi deserves credit for urging his compatriots to overcome the much-neglected malaise of the lack of cleanliness and sanitation in India.

There are some other positives. Modi has announced his intention to strengthen cooperative federalism by harmonizing Centre-state relations. On a grandiose note he has declared: 'Team India = Prime Minister + Chief Ministers'. This shows that he envisages a more important role for the heads of governments in India's twenty-nine states, several of which are bigger in population than many countries in the world. He has promised devolution of greater financial powers to state governments. However, the fruits of this welcome new approach have not become visible yet. Part of the reason for this is the unfortunate habit of ruling and opposition parties to not cooperate with each other in important development matters. When he was the chief minister of Gujarat, Modi had rightly protested against excessive concentration of powers in the hands of the central government. Another chief minister, J. Jayalalithaa of Tamil Nadu, had even stated, when the Congress-led United Progressive Alliance (UPA) was in power at the Centre, that New Delhi had reduced state governments to the level of 'municipal corporations'. Now, as prime minister, Modi has the duty to repair this unbalanced relationship.

FOREIGN POLICY: NORMALIZATION OF INDIA-PAKISTAN RELATIONS IS THE HARDEST TEST – AND THE BIGGEST OPPORTUNITY – FOR MODI

Modi's performance on the foreign policy front so far has been creditworthy. He has taken personal charge of introducing dynamism into India's relations with the rest of the world. He has visited more countries in the first twenty months of his prime ministership than any of his predecessors in a comparable period. This is a highly welcome effort, even though Modi's political opponents have wrongly criticized him for spending too much time on his foreign travels. India must play a prominent role on the global stage as befits its size, ambition, responsibility and civilizational standing. Today India's profile has become higher both in the Western world and also in our immediate and extended cultural neighbourhood. India's relations with China, the emerging great power, have significantly improved even though there is no resolution in sight for the border dispute between the two countries. In an interview to *Time* magazine in May 2015, Modi rightly pointed out: 'Not a single bullet has been fired for over a quarter of a century now. This essentially goes to prove that both countries, India and China, have learnt from history.'

The only country with which Modi has so far failed to improve relations is Pakistan. Indeed, inconsistency and confusion, coupled with needless bravado, have marked his government's approach to Pakistan. Normalization of India-Pakistan relations is a historical necessity for both countries – indeed, for South Asia as a whole. Both New Delhi and Islamabad need to revise their traditional, and failed, approaches to dealing with one another as enemies. Vajpayee and Advani had made a bold attempt to follow a creative and unorthodox path to mending relations with Pakistan. They met with difficulties and failures. However, sincere failures are the building blocks of success, if the purpose is worthy.

After spending nearly one and a half years in deciding how to engage Pakistan, Modi sprang a pleasant surprise by paying an unexpected visit to Lahore on 25 December 2015. Although the specific purpose of his visit was to greet his counterpart Nawaz Sharif on his birthday, Modi's gesture signalled a much-needed thaw in India-Pakistan relations. It was widely welcomed on both sides of the border, including Modi's critics. The two prime ministers have also decided to resume bilateral talks between India and Pakistan, rechristened as 'Comprehensive Bilateral Dialogue', which is meant to cover all the outstanding issues between the two countries, including the knotty Kashmir dispute. This is a highly welcome decision. If the two sides decide to walk along the path of dialogue, with the requisite quantum of mutual trust, determination and spirit of accommodation, they are bound to succeed.

Of course, the road ahead for the 'Comprehensive Bilateral Dialogue' is by no means smooth. There will be many obstacles and crises along the way. One such crisis erupted when both India and Pakistan were still basking in the warmth of Modi's visit to Lahore. In the first week of January 2016, Pakistan-based terrorists, reportedly belonging to Jaish-e-Mohammed, attacked the Indian Air Force base in Pathankot in Punjab. Seven security personnel were killed in the attack, which naturally outraged the Indian public. It also temporarily led to the postponement of the scheduled meeting between the foreign secretaries of the two countries. However, such terrorist attacks are only to be expected. Whenever Indian and Pakistani governments have decided to begin serious bilateral talks, anti-India elements in Pakistan have tried to sabotage them in some or the other violent way. Stopping the talks for this reason would amount to victory for those who want India and Pakistan to continue to live as hostile neighbours. Therefore, the test of Modi's leadership – and also the test of his counterpart in Pakistan – lies in his determination to continue the talks in an uninterrupted, meaningful and result-oriented manner, certain in the knowledge that dialogue is the only way to resolve all the problems between our two countries. There is simply no military solution.

In case Modi has internalized this realization, he will have to take up two attendant tasks. First, he has to courageously reject the advice of both the militaristic establishment in New Delhi as well as the rabid Pakistan-haters in the Sangh Parivar. Without lowering the guard in the uncompromising fight against terrorism, he has to remould the thinking of the Sangh Parivar in favour of an enduring rapprochement with Pakistan on terms that are honourable and acceptable to both sides. Specifically, and this is the second task, both he and the Sangh Parivar have to recognize the truth that any formula for normalization of relations between India and Pakistan has to address the core issue of Jammu & Kashmir. As per the Simla Pact of 1972, both countries have accepted that a 'final settlement' of the Jammu & Kashmir issue is yet to be reached, and also that they would settle it through bilateral negotiations. Obviously, this requires, both in India and in Pakistan, broad national consensus and the willingness to accept certain compromises. So far at least, Modi has not articulated his thinking on the resolution of the Kashmir issue, without which normalization of India-Pakistan relations can at best be partial and tentative.

On its part, the army and the political establishment in Pakistan also must show courage and determination in fighting the forces of Islamist extremism and terrorism. Correcting their costly mistakes in the past, they must vow never again to use or allow these murderous forces to target India. After all, they ought to know that Pakistan itself has suffered the most on account of encouraging and sheltering extremist and terrorist organizations on its soil.

MODI, THE MEDIA AND HIS COMMUNICATION WITH THE PEOPLE

An important factor that contributed to Modi's spectacular victory in 2014 was his high-voltage campaign and communication. He is a smart communicator, a leader who knows how to use the media to his advantage. The ten-year rule of Manmohan Singh, whom Modi succeeded, was a period when India had the most non-communicative prime minister in its history. Against that backdrop, Modi knows the power of communication and is adept at using it in innovative ways. While comparison with Singh's relationship with the media is unavoidable, it must be seen in perspective. He was not a leader in his own right. He was also by nature shy and unenthusiastic about communicating with, and through, the media. In contrast, Modi is a mass leader. Mastery over mass communication is a professional requirement for him and also something he revels in, as is evident in his adept use of the social media.

This is also evident in the novelty of his direct, and frequent, communication with the people after becoming prime minister. Example: his 'Mann Ki Baat' broadcasts on All India Radio, which still has huge reach in rural India. Through these broadcasts, he has attempted to articulate his thoughts, concerns and convictions on important societal issues such as girls' education and the need to prevent female infanticide, which has a disastrous effect on gender parity in the population in several states in India. The necessity and usefulness of prime ministers' forceful communication with the people on such issues cannot be belittled. After all, India's prime ministers are not just heads of governments, they are not CEOs of a governing establishment; rather, they are the leaders of the world's largest democracy that is facing gigantic social and developmental problems. These problems can be effectively tackled only through a strong partnership between the people and the government.

While such innovations are welcome, an obvious area of weakness in the Modi government's communication strategy is that it has got excessively personalized by the prime minister himself. Barring a few senior ministers, other voices in the government are hardly being heard. Even these senior ministers are not engaged in communicating the government's vision. They stick only to the nitty-gritty of their work. If this situation is not corrected in Modi's remaining years in office, his government's efficacy and public image will surely be affected. Questions are already being raised, both by media persons and well-informed sections of the public, about the performance of many ministers and ministries.

For effective governance in a country as large and diverse as India, Modi should not carry the entire burden of good performance of his government, and the credible communication of its policies and programmes, on his own shoulders. No prime minister, howsoever powerful or capable, can succeed in such efforts. For any team to win, the captain must no doubt play well and lead from the front. But he alone cannot ensure his team's victory. How the team as a whole performs matters. On this criterion, the Modi government's first year in office serves as a poor benchmark for its remaining four years.

Soon after Modi's spectacular victory in 2014, there were apprehensions that his government would not tolerate criticism in the media and hence curb the freedom of the press. These apprehensions have largely receded. This is primarily on account of the intrinsic strength of the Indian media and the spirit of press freedom that is deeply rooted in Indian democracy. The Indian media has not yet turned critical of the prime minister himself. However, criticism of the functioning of his government and, especially, of the BJP governments in certain states, is rising sharply. Inappropriate conduct of some his ministerial and party colleagues, and scandals involving a few chief ministers, are sullying the image of the BJP – and, by extension, also that of the prime minister since he is now the sole face of the ruling party. Questions are also being asked about dissonant, and often dangerous, voices from the champions of Hindutva (Hindu supremacist) ideology who support the Modi government.

So far, the government has not acted in a vindictive manner, which is how it should be. Modi made some reassuring statements in his interview to *Time* magazine in May 2015 by affirming that 'democracy is in India's DNA', thereby acknowledging that freedom of the press is also in India's DNA. He said that India's progress could be ensured only through an 'innate belief in democracy' and not through 'dictatorship' or by a 'powerful person who believes in concentrating power at one place'. Nevertheless, plurality of views in the Indian media, and the unfettered freedom to express them, must be defended constantly by vigilant sections of our society, journalists included.

And this also applies to the defence of secularism, which is the bedrock of our democracy and a guarantor of India's unity and integrity.

MODI'S DISCOMFITURE WITH SECULARISM AND ITS IMPLICATIONS FOR THE IDEA OF INDIA

It is in the area of safeguarding secularism that Modi, his party and his government have a lot of work to do to allay the concerns and misgivings of not only India's religious minorities but also of secular-minded Hindus who constitute the majority within India's majority community. Modi would surely be inviting trouble for himself if he chose not to remove these concerns. After all, his failure or unwillingness to do so would seriously threaten the Idea of India that guarantees our national unity and integrity. And no leader, howsoever powerful, can govern India if his core beliefs and policies endanger the Idea of India; if he or she alienates the country's large population of religious minorities, especially Muslims.

What is the Idea of India? Why is it so fundamental to our national identity, unity, survival and progress?

India is, and has always been, a multi-faith nation. Freedom of religion, equality of all faiths in the eyes of the nation-state and all its institutions, equal respect for all faiths both in polity and society, and non-discrimination on the basis of creed or caste have been assured by the Indian Constitution. They are also embedded in India's age-old cultural and civilizational heritage, which celebrates unity in diversity. They together constitute the meaning of secularism in the Indian context. The Partition of India in 1947 and the carving out of Pakistan as a separate 'Muslim nation' on the basis of the spurious Two-Nation theory dealt a severe blow to this heritage. In subsequent decades, this Muslim nation further solidified its identity as an Islamic nation. The population of Hindus, Sikhs and Christians in Pakistan shrank drastically. Their rights were severely curtailed. However, as far as the truncated post-1947 India is concerned, the founding fathers of our republic wisely desisted from making India a Hindu version of Pakistan; they created a Constitution that committed India to the principle of secularism.

It is true that the word 'secularism' was not explicitly included in the Preamble of the Indian Constitution when it came into force in 1950. Opponents of secularism, most of whom are in the Sangh Parivar, often gripe over the fact that the word was incorporated into the Constitution as a preambular principle only later in 1976, when India was reeling under the Emergency rule (1975-1977) imposed by the then prime minister, Indira Gandhi. Their criticism does not hold water for two reasons. First, even though the word 'secular' was not specifically used to describe the Republic of India in 1950, the content and essence of even the original unamended version of the Indian Constitution was incontrovertibly secular. Secondly, no political party, not even the BJP, has demanded, after the lifting of the Emergency, that the Constitution should be amended once again to excise the word 'secular' from its Preamble. In fact, the Janata Party government, which came into being in 1977 – both Vajpayee and Advani were prominent ministers in that government – annulled all the anti-democracy amendments to the Constitution that had been passed by Indira Gandhi's regime during the Emergency. However, it kept the word 'secular' intact in the Preamble. This means that, both in the post-1950 period as well as in the post-1976 period, there has been a rock-solid national consensus on secularism as a fundamental pillar of the Idea of India.

Sadly, this consensus is sought to be broken, altered, or at any rate weakened by the BJP and its government now. Concerns on this score have arisen because of the Sangh Parivar's extreme discomfort with the secular core of the constitutionally endorsed Idea of India. In open defiance of the spirit and the text of the Indian Constitution, leaders of the RSS and the Vishwa Hindu Parishad (VHP), an affiliate of the RSS, have been saying more vociferously than ever before that India should be declared a Hindu Rashtra. This clearly means that, in their understanding of India, non-Hindus – especially, Muslims who constitute the largest minority in the country – have a secondary status which is not on a par with the Hindus'. When pressed to explain their position, RSS ideologues state that the word 'Hindu', according to them, connotes culture and not religion, and therefore even Muslims in India should regard themselves as culturally 'Hindus'.

RSS HAIR-SPLITTING

This is nothing but deceptive verbal hair-splitting and conceptual obfuscation. By no stretch of imagination can the word 'Hindu' be stripped of its religious connotation in today's India. Indeed, when the VHP describes itself as an organization of Hindus worldwide, it clearly uses the term 'Hindu' in its religious sense. All the religious leaders who congregate on the VHP platform are Hindu religious leaders; it has no place for Muslim or Christian religious leaders.

Obviously, the claim that India is a 'Hindu Rashtra' is an assault on India as a secular nation. The claim is deeply offensive to Muslim, Christian and other non-Hindu Indians. Indeed, it also offends the patriotism of a majority of Hindus who are secular by nature.

A quick explanation is in order here even at the risk of a slight digression. It might be asked: If a majority of Hindus are secular, how did the BJP under Modi's leadership manage to secure a decisive mandate in the 2014 parliamentary election? The answer to this question is that most of the Hindus who voted for the BJP – Muslims hardly ever vote for the BJP in significant numbers – did so not because they were influenced by the Sangh Parivar's Hindutva ideology. They did so principally because, firstly, they wanted to end the highly unpopular Congress rule which was marred by many corruption scandals; secondly, they were influenced by Modi's promise of ushering in development and better governance; thirdly, Modi was able to project himself as a 'strong leader'; fourthly, the Congress party's new and young leader Rahul Gandhi failed hopelessly to match Modi's mass appeal; and fifthly, both Hindus and Muslims were disenchanted with the Congress party's self-serving and inconsistent espousal of secularism. Those who voted for the BJP solely because of its Hindutva ideology were only its core voters, whose number is small and who, by themselves, can never bring their party to power either in central or state elections.

Let us return to the discussion on secularism. In a clear sign that the RSS was tightening its ideological control over the BJP, after the end of the Vajpayee-Advani era, the word 'secularism' did not find even a cursory mention in the BJP's manifesto for the 2014 parliamentary election. This was not an oversight. Modi himself, as the party's prime ministerial candidate, had shown his disapproval of the word 'secularism'. In an interview given to Shahid Siddiqui before the polls, while answering a pointed question *'Will you keep secularism as part of the Constitution or remove it?'* Modi described secularism as an 'imported' word.

The answer given by India's would-be prime minister was as baffling as it was disturbing. Secularism, understood as a non-theocratic state that shows equal respect for all faiths, is by no means an imported concept. If Modi thinks secularism is foreign to India, he should also declare parliamentary democracy to be foreign to India since it too is 'imported' from the West!

It is worth emphasizing here that BJP's own constitution, adopted when the party was founded in 1980 with Vajpayee as its founding president, shows allegiance to 'secularism'. If Prime Minister Modi believes that it is an 'imported' concept, will he now get his party to remove the word from its constitution? Even if he does, he and his supporters should know that 'secularism' cannot be removed from the Preamble to India's Constitution since it forms part of the 'Basic Structure' of the Constitution. The Supreme Court has clearly, and wisely, curtailed Parliament's powers, under Article 368, to amend the Constitution when such amendment seeks to alter its very heart and soul. The basic structure can be changed only by a new Constituent

Assembly. Neither the BJP nor any other party can bring a new Constituent Assembly into being.

Nevertheless, the prime minister's displeasure over 'secularism' has helped create an intellectual atmosphere in which many of his supporters have taken to secularism bashing with no fear of being reprimanded. For example, the social media is awash with the abusive term 'sickular' to describe the secular constituency.

To be fair to Modi, I must add here that in the same pre-election interview with Shahid Siddiqui, he had also spoken these reassuring words: 'There is only one holy book for the Indian government, and that is the Constitution. I respect everything that the Constitution says.' He is therefore duty-bound, and also bound by his own solemn assurance, to swear his allegiance to secularism. In practical and policy terms, this obliges him and his government to treat all religions and religious communities equally with no discrimination. His own party's pre-election promise of 'Sabka Saath, Sabka Vikas' enjoins him to do so.

THE COMING TENSION BETWEEN MODI AND THE SANGH PARIVAR – WILL THERE BE A 'POINT OF RETURN'?

An important question arises here. As the prime minister of India, Modi has to scrupulously follow the Indian Constitution's commandment on secularism. His failure to do so will be the undoing of his premiership. Whether he likes it or not, whether his core beliefs permit him or not, he is bound by the Constitution to ensure that his government does nothing that violates secular ideals and principles. Which means that his government cannot follow a majoritarian agenda, even though that is what many in the Sangh Parivar would like it to do. The prime minister's fairness and rectitude would be especially tested if, God forbid, India witnesses an outbreak of communal violence. The communal violence in Gujarat in 2002 was certainly a blot on his record as the state's chief minister. Indeed, it was also a blot on Vajpayee's prime ministership, besides being a major cause for his failure to lead the BJP to win a renewed mandate in the 2004 Lok Sabha election.

It is obvious, therefore, that Modi and his government – and also BJP governments in states as well as the BJP organization all over the country – must ensure zero tolerance both for communal violence and terrorist violence. Those guilty of aiding and abetting such violence, irrespective of their religious and political affiliation, must be punished as per the rule of law.

Zero tolerance for communal violence also entails no tolerance for communal and hate propaganda by Hindu, Muslim or other organizations. Naturally, this includes the RSS propaganda that India is – and should be declared as – a 'Hindu Rashtra'. So far, no BJP leader, not even Modi, has publicly criticized the RSS for this divisive advocacy even though some BJP leaders privately express reservations about the 'Hindu Rashtra' concept. However, with the passage of time, Modi and his colleagues in the government and the party will be forced to distance themselves from, and also actively curb, the anti-Muslim and anti-minorities propaganda by the outfits of the Sangh Parivar. They will also have to show at least some concern for the legitimate concerns, needs and demands of the Muslim community, even at the risk of being accused by Hindu communalists of following the 'Congress policy of appeasing Muslims'. Modi is an astute politician and he knows that alienating a large section of the Indian population would create problems for his premiership – especially for his desire to win a second term in the parliamentary election in 2019.

All this will inevitably create tension between Modi and the Sangh Parivar. When such tension surfaces, the choices before him would be stark: either he allows himself and his government to be controlled by the Sangh Parivar, or he curbs and subdues the Sangh Parivar in pursuit of its majoritarian agenda. The former choice will spell doom for his government. Of course, there could also be other threats to his government such as failure to fulfil people's expectations and its own election promises related to development and good governance. If Modi makes the latter choice, he would be doing a big service to India.

In my opinion, making the latter choice – acceptance of the secular anchor of the Idea of India – would constitute for Modi and the BJP 'the point of return' to the mainstream of national life.

Whether Modi and the BJP actually make this choice or not is difficult to predict but not beyond the pale of possibility. After all, there are many sensible and secular-minded people in the RSS and the BJP who care for India's future and who would be amenable to revising their own ideological beliefs. Electoral compulsions and the compulsions of retaining power will also force them to change their convictions, policies and conduct.

After all, India's democracy and our plural cultural-civilizational heritage have the invincible power to ensure that only those who are, or become, faithful to the Idea of India will govern this great nation and shape its destiny. In that power lies the hope for India.

Collapse of the Congress

Zoya Hasan

꩜

Zoya Hasan is professor emeritus, Centre for Political Studies, Jawaharlal Nehru University.

The 2014 general elections marked a tectonic shift in Indian politics. For the first time since independence, India elected a right-wing party with a majority. Even though there have been bigger electoral landmarks in the past, this election stood out because Narendra Modi led the Bharatiya Janata Party (BJP) and the National Democratic Alliance (NDA) to a sensational win. Its victory was so complete that it captured all or most of the seats in some states and reduced the Indian National Congress to forty-four of the 543 in the Lok Sabha – a shocking comedown for the party whose history is integral to India's founding narrative. Congress polled just 19.3 per cent of the votes, declining from 28.6 per cent in the 2009 election.

Election 2014 saw a shift in outcomes, processes and personalities. This is the first time since 1984 that any party has won a majority for

.

itself in the Lok Sabha. The BJP won 282 seats and 31 per cent of the national vote. Its main success came from the states of north and west India, with the party winning four of every five seats it contested. Its ability to garner a substantial Hindu vote in Uttar Pradesh and Bihar through communal polarization paved its way to an absolute majority in the Lok Sabha. Never before had so much money been spent in fighting an election as in this one. The BJP received massive support from the corporate sector and easily outspent its rivals. This election also saw an extraordinary rise in media power with real politics done in TV studios and social media. It was the most personality-driven election with Modi deliberately turning a parliamentary election into a presidential-style one.

Today, the Congress stands decimated. For more than three quarters of a century it dominated Indian politics. It is now without a strong base anywhere, having been completely wiped out in Tamil Nadu and Andhra Pradesh, made no headway in Telangana despite the decision to bifurcate Andhra, weakened in Karnataka, defeated in Maharashtra, marginalized in Uttar Pradesh and West Bengal, and has drawn a near blank in most key states across the Hindi heartland. It did not win a single seat in Delhi, Gujarat, Goa, Himachal Pradesh, Odisha, Jharkhand, Rajasthan, Tamil Nadu and Uttarakhand. It lost the assembly elections in Haryana, Maharashtra and Chhattisgarh held in October 2014. In Punjab, it is facing a serious threat from the Aam Aadmi Party (AAP). In Delhi, it has virtually disappeared. It failed to open its account in the 2015 Delhi Legislative Assembly elections perhaps for the first time in its history. It has lost its entire base to the AAP. Of the seventy candidates who contested elections to the Delhi Legislative Assembly, sixty-three lost their security deposits, including Ajay Maken, the chief of the campaign committee. More significantly, it is in no position to call the shots in the key states of Bihar, Uttar Pradesh, West Bengal, Tamil Nadu, Maharashtra, Andhra Pradesh and Telangana.

The defeat of the Congress in the general elections in 2014 was far worse than anything in its long history. Indeed, its decimation everywhere in this election constitutes the most serious crisis for the party, worse even than the late 1970s after Indira Gandhi had suspended democracy. The Congress failure to win a single seat in Delhi only confirmed the existential crisis facing the party after it lost power at the Centre. Congress leader Jairam Ramesh rightly observed: 'Our electoral debacle has been much deeper than we expected and the demoralization is increased because of the successive defeats we have had in the state elections.'[1] Yet, its top leaders have barely spoken after the defeat. Sonia Gandhi and Rahul Gandhi accepted personal responsibility for the defeat and offered to resign at the Congress Working Committee meeting immediately after the elections, but the party shielded them, rejecting their resignations.

The Congress faces a structural dilemma on several fronts: organizational weakness, ideological stagnation and shrinking social support.[2] At one time, it was a democratic party with a formidable organization that ran an effective political machine, distributing patronage in exchange for electoral support. From the 1970s onwards, party organization in most states degenerated severely. This was mainly because Indira Gandhi, who had very little use for the institutional structure of the party, made systematic efforts to change it into a centralized and family-centred political organization. From then on no attention was given to the reorganization and regeneration of the Congress. There is no evidence whatsoever that the party was able to use its stint in power to energize the organization. Instead, for the last ten years, it has not allowed strong regional leadership to grow and consolidate. Even after the defeat, its leadership has done nothing to arrest the steep decline and hasn't initiated any mass mobilization to revive the party or take up any issue that can truly galvanize an Opposition or demonstrated an interest in building alliances. The big question is whether the Congress can recover and reorganize its forces, ideas and energies after this devastating defeat.

UPA'S RECORD

The BJP issued a booklet condemning United Progressive Alliance (UPA) prime minister Manmohan Singh's ten years as a 'Dark Decade in Governance',[3] and media commentators routinely described it as a 'wasted decade'[4] or 'India's lost decade'.[5] This has become so much a part of common discourse that we ignore some of the big ideas of the UPA, specially the UPA-1 government, which enhanced the welfare of many. Despite economic slowdown and inflation, there was an enormous expansion of well-being over the last decade. The people are far better off than they were at the turn of the millennium.[6] Poverty declined faster than at any time in India's history.[7] The poverty ratio declined by at least 15 percentage points.[8] Between 2004–05 and 2009–10 – the initial years of UPA rule – the gap between rich and poor shrunk appreciably, as 40 per cent of the population experienced upward mobility.[9] Over these years, some 15 per cent of the total population or 40 per cent of the poor in India moved above the poverty line.

Even though neo-liberal policies were never given up, the UPA-1 did promote a range of social welfare measures and programmes. The government took advantage of high economic growth and the revenue it generated to pilot several welfare measures that enshrine a new set of socio-economic entitlements through legally enforceable rights. These rights were not abstract but extended to the day-to-day survival of marginal groups. Although the programmes' purpose was to compensate the poor for the deprivations they suffer under neo-liberal policies, they do signify an emphasis on state as an instrument for redistribution and social change. Programmes like the Mahatma Gandhi National Rural Employment Guarantee Act (MGNREGA), Sarva Shiksha Abhiyan (SSA), Right to Education, National Rural

Health Mission (NRHM), the Forest Rights Act, etc., tried to make overall economic growth more inclusive under UPA-1.

But the Congress failed to capitalize on the momentum of the change achieved under UPA-1. Its political support began to erode with the economic slowdown in the last two years of its second term. On the face of it, the UPA-2's problems on the economy were surprising, given that economic growth was at its strongest during the UPA's tenure, as compared to previous governments, though it declined significantly since 2010. Manmohan Singh, in his Independence Day speech as prime minister on 15 August 2013, blamed the global economic crisis for the domestic slowdown. But the government couldn't really blame external factors or internal political instability for the crisis which was actually a reflection of its own mismanagement.[10] While the global recession did slow down growth, most of the factors contributing to it were actually domestic in nature. In fact, the slowdown was linked to the neo-liberal growth model itself which entails giving preference in everything from cheap credit to captive power to big business. It ended up promoting a crony capitalist system.

Economic expansion was driven by an investment boom helped by access to land and natural resources in return for pay-offs to politicians. Elite capture was palpable in the sweetheart deals between political and economic elites in mining, land acquisition and telecommunications. The investment subsidy implicit in underpricing of assets became unsustainable after the escalation of protests against the public acquisition of land for private purposes and corruption scandals.[11] The debate during the election indicated that the intrinsic relationship between crony capitalism and corruption was a major concern for the public. However, crony capitalism is not a new phenomenon, it has a long history in India and various parties and governments have promoted it, most notably the Congress in its previous stints in government. It was a striking feature of the Modi government in Gujarat as well but these charges did not stick. In the case of the Congress, it was the sheer scale of corruption at the Centre for which the Congress had to take the blame. The resulting yearning for change due to this and other shortcomings in performance sealed the Congress's fate.[12]

Another major trigger for the Congress collapse was unrelenting inflation, the highest in twenty years, which turned the poor and the middle class against the party. This triggered people's anger and disenchantment and a strong desire for change. As the economic boom faded, the enthusiasm for welfare measures waned, leading to dilution in public support. The pullback on social sector programmes added to the deepening political crisis enveloping the Congress as it began losing the support of the poor who had helped it to rise from 141 seats in 2004 to 206 in the 2009 elections.

The implementation of rights-based programmes under UPA-2 was very patchy. Strong attempts were made by the government to limit the scope of MGNREGA wages which were still not paid. It had become less important as its budgets were reduced in the name of targeted delivery, cash transfers and reducing subsidies. The Congress promised to enact legislation to ensure a minimum quantity of affordable food to all poor households in the country, if it was voted back to power. But the government took five years to enact the National Food Security Act (NFSA). It did push ahead with the food bill in the twilight of its second term, but it was not easy to do in the last six months what could have been done in the first six. Since it was passed by Parliament only in September 2013, the UPA could not implement it. As a result, it didn't get any political benefit out of it. Both these landmark programmes suffered because of differences within the government on coverage and quantum of support. The dithering and vacillation on some of these social legislations was certainly a factor in the failure to retain the support of the poor. Just as the increase in the spread of social programmes under UPA-1 was a factor in the electoral victory of 2009, so it is likely that the poor showing under UPA-2 added to public unhappiness with the government. This combined with a decade of jobless growth created eddies of discontent which was difficult to control.

As against the half-heartedness of the Congress on both the growth and redistributive fronts, Modi offered the electorate decisive action and the clarity of the Gujarat model which is as neo-liberal as is possible in India: growth through private investment and good infrastructure and easy access to land and natural resources. Modi's image as a pro-business leader provided a clear alternative to the UPA's model driven by social policy.[13] He was the first leader in independent India who spelt out a vision for promoting prosperity rather than combating poverty. Needless to say, in his election campaign, the word inequality wasn't heard even once. Instead, throughout the campaign, there was talk of spurring economic growth and facilitating ease of business which will do more to improve opportunities than more public spending on social welfare measures. This is just what the corporate sector and the aspirational middle class wanted to hear. This is perhaps why there was the near-unanimous condemnation of the right to food as profligate.[14] The NFSA was strongly attacked as an instance of irresponsible populism and frittering away of resources that will destroy the growth story forever. The idea that India cannot afford food security but can afford to give duty exemptions to keep gold imports out of the tax net illustrates the new politics which has come to dominate economic thinking.[15]

TURNING POINT

The Congress party and its government lost control of the narrative in 2011, the year the anti-corruption movement took place, causing an eruption of public anger against the scam-tainted government. While the UPA government may have been able to disperse the crowds from the streets then, it could not really rid itself of the core charge that the protesters were making: that the Congress-led UPA-2 government was perhaps the most corrupt in independent India. The explosion of revelations about corrupt practices pointed to the worst excesses of crony capitalism that underpinned the growth story. Yet, Manmohan Singh and Sonia Gandhi did not come out and assure the country that they would crack down on graft. Both of them hardly spoke to the public and the media. While the government kept silent, the BJP carried out a high-pitched political propaganda against the mega corruption of the UPA-2 government. What's more, Singh's unwillingness to explain and communicate made the UPA come through as a regime that was not only corrupt and unaccountable but also arrogant and indifferent to feedback and criticism as well.

The anti-corruption movement hit the credibility of the government by questioning its legitimacy. In 2011, the Congress could have reached out to anti-corruption campaigners but didn't. This was a turning point in cementing hostility towards the Congress. While in 2011, the fallout of the movement was difficult to gauge as elections were still three years away, it was clear even then that the government had alienated vast swathes of voters across the social divide, and earned the wrath of the middle classes and young men and women voters of the future. It culminated in its colossal defeat at the hands of the BJP, and not the AAP, which was born out of the anti-corruption movement. However, AAP had a big hand in the BJP's win because its members played a central role in the movement that delegitimized the Congress. Furthermore, AAP had routed the Congress in the 2013 assembly elections; the party never recovered from this rout. The BJP was undoubtedly the beneficiary of the bumper anti-Congress harvest that the India Against Corruption (IAC) movement and AAP sowed.

On the whole, both the government and the party were beleaguered throughout the five years of the second term. Manmohan Singh ran a government with multiple power centres. The leadership vacuum was such that no one's was the last word in the government or the party. An important reason for this was differences within the Congress and between the party and government. There were conflicting positions in the party and government on most issues – notably, the Indo-US nuclear deal, land acquisition, foreign direct investment in multi-brand retail and, more generally, neo-liberal economic reforms. The rift seems to have begun with the Women's Reservation Bill when Sonia Gandhi first goaded and then directed a reluctant government to ensure its passage in the Rajya Sabha, despite obvious political risks. This was followed later by her party leaders virtually stalling the Nuclear Civil Liability Bill, which was threatening to become a sensitive issue as it seemed to protect American commercial interests than address Indian safety concerns.

The Congress remained deeply divided with regard to the strategy for economic growth. Two dominant positions were discernible on the way forward. One was a nebulous social democratic platform supported by Sonia Gandhi that shares misgivings with regard to neo-liberal economic reforms, favours an accommodative approach towards the marginalized and the poor, and believes such a position helps to differentiate and distance itself from the BJP. The other side led by Manmohan Singh and P. Chidambaram, including many other senior leaders in the party, favoured the neo-liberal position with its emphasis on high GDP growth, fiscal consolidation and economic reforms to push growth. The core issue was the conflict between those who advocated speeding up economic reforms as a way of restoring high growth and those who swear by social welfare necessary for inclusive growth.

LEADERSHIP CRISIS

Leadership was a major issue for voters in the 2014 elections. Modern mass politics demands visible leadership from the front, not the assertion of authority by remote control. Voters believe strong decisive leadership can solve the country's numerous problems. The leadership issue became critical as the BJP made the election more personal with

Modi continuously attacking 'family' politics, and the Gandhi family in particular. However, the Gandhi family was in decline long before the Modi attacks.[16] Be that as it may, it is difficult to separate the party from the Gandhis. The 2014 verdict made clear that leadership in India is not a family entitlement and voters are increasingly less deferential to family privilege. Moreover, Rahul Gandhi demonstrated his inability to generate support on the campaign trail. He said the right things but failed to connect with the voters; he did not address them in an idiom that holds much appeal for them. Evidently, he was diffident about power and position, and showed no appetite for a political fight.[17] Even within his own party there were 'doubts about the capability and willingness of Rahul Gandhi to provide a hands-on leadership to the party'.[18] He was 'the leader who won't lead', as one TV anchor put it,[19] in sharp contrast to Modi who was overeager to lead and dominate.

Rahul Gandhi was expected to assume a larger responsibility in the party's affairs after the electoral debacle. But he didn't. His reluctance was apparent from the Karnataka Congress leader Mallikarjun Kharge's appointment as the parliamentary party leader in the Lok Sabha in the aftermath of the defeat. As the *Hindu* editorial, after the Congress party scored a zero in the 2015 Delhi Legislative Assembly elections, put it, 'He does not have what it takes: he has neither demonstrated the ability to sustain an idea or the hard work demanded of a full-time politician in a leadership role.'[20]

The failure of leadership in the Lok Sabha election and in a series of state assembly elections before and after it is patently obvious; yet, the party's confidence in the Gandhis remains unchanged. Their authority and supremacy have not been seriously challenged within the party. Thus, despite repeated electoral failures there is a demand for Rahul Gandhi's elevation as the president of the Congress party. But the challenges facing Gandhi appear far too numerous for any politician to tackle single-handedly.[21]

IDEOLOGICAL DRIFT

Apart from the leadership crisis, two other issues were important. These pertained to the ideology and policies of the party, and reform and reorganization of the party. The Congress never had a clear-cut ideology like most other catch-all parties. Yet, its identity is rooted in a left-of-centre platform which it betrayed by flirting with neo-liberalism and indulging in crony capitalism. Besides, as mentioned above, the Congress kept moving back and forth between a pro-poor distributive policies and neo-liberal policies which left its supporters confused. This equivocation was apparent in December 2013 when Rahul Gandhi tried to placate big businesses and dispel the swelling criticism, by both industrialists and the Opposition, by highlighting the strong connect between the Congress and the Indian industry. He told a gathering at the Federation of Indian Chambers of Commerce and Industry (FICCI) that members of the industry are 'stakeholders of the Congress party', and that he had removed an obstacle to growth by changing the minister (Jayanthi Natarajan), who had in the perception of businessmen delayed environmental clearances.[22] However, a year later, in February 2015, he said: 'Let me make it very clear ... I don't do politics for industrialists. I do politics for the poor and will continue to fight for their rights.'[23]

With each successive spell out of power, the party's ability to retain its supporters has dwindled. The rainbow started to fade from the early 1990s, especially in the post-Mandal period. By the late 1990s, the famous Congress system had all but vanished. While it once embraced a broad spectrum of social groups across the country under its capacious umbrella, the attempt to recreate a social coalition through inclusive development did not produce a sustainable social base. It has lost its wide appeal across the country, as powerful caste and community groupings have voted for regional and smaller parties. The problem is that the rich and the poor, the upper castes and the lower castes, and the minorities, all are angry with the Congress. Ironically, even as the party has lost ground with the middle classes, it has also lost the support of Dalits, Adivasis and Muslims to regional parties. In short, the Congress is left with no distinct group to turn to for support. To regain its influence, it needs decentralization and it needs to build broad-based social coalitions at the state level. Strong, locally rooted state leaders could improve its political prospects, which in turn can spread to national politics.

As for party reform, it is a well-known fact that the Congress is a much depleted grass-roots organization in need of a complete revamp. For nearly a decade, Rahul Gandhi has focused his political capital on the long-term project of trying to democratize the party organization.[24] But his efforts have neither produced any discernible change in the organization nor delivered a new crop of leaders. So far his efforts to introduce inner-party democracy have not worked either because he has not put his heart into it or is stymied by senior leaders because they fear that it will end up marginalizing them.

A series of discussions after the massive election defeat has led neither to a plan of action, nor reorganization of the party.[25] A committee, headed by former defence minister A.K. Antony, was appointed by Sonia Gandhi to investigate the causes of the defeat.[26] It absolved the party's top leadership of any blame.[27] The committee submitted its report to Sonia Gandhi which was not shared with the members of the party. While submitting the report, Antony said that 'the reasons for the Congress defeat were something else'.[28]

BOTCHED CAMPAIGN

As a final point, the Congress ran a lacklustre campaign which clearly failed to connect with the new generation of voters who are no longer bound by traditional affiliations to a family or an ideology. It was no match for the BJP's well-crafted nationwide campaign against UPA's misrule and Congress ineptitude, creating a public mood in favour of the BJP as the preferred agent of change. The Congress campaign appeared to be weak, directionless and disjointed, and constantly played catch-up rather than defining the political narrative. At the meeting just a few weeks after the defeat, Sonia Gandhi singled out the party's communications strategy as one of its major failures, saying that 'the message of Congress was lost in the din and dust raised by an aggressive and polarizing campaign by our opponents, which was backed by unlimited resources and a hostile media'.[29] But it is the Congress and the UPA parties who are to blame for this as they hardly publicized the welfare measures either because of a lack of conviction in them or because of the feeling that they had not lived up to their own promises.

The BJP's slick campaign, bankrolled by corporate India, was unprecedented.[30] The grass-roots efforts of the nationwide branches of the RSS and its affiliated organizations, enthused by Modi who was one of their own, helped convert a groundswell of dissatisfaction with the Congress into a wave. But Modi, for his part, aimed his barbs at a single target: the Gandhi family which he took to task for everything that had gone wrong in the country. By turning the campaign into a highly personalized one, he put them on the defensive.[31] That only lent greater credence to Modi's claim that to realize its full potential India had to get rid of the Gandhi dynasty and make India a 'Congress-mukt Bharat' (Congress-free India).

His ascent was undoubtedly powered by a pliant media which was deftly used by the BJP to create a 'Modi wave'. Its media blitzkrieg dominated electoral politics as the media became its main campaign platform. For weeks, any speech by Modi in any remote district ran live on several channels. A study by the Centre for Media Studies found that Modi dominated over a third of the prime-time news telecast on five major channels. From 1 to 11 May 2014, Modi's time crossed the 50 per cent mark. Over six times what Rahul Gandhi got. And ten times the share of AAP leader Arvind Kejriwal.[32] The phenomenon of paid news acquired a new dimension altogether with media houses under pressure to act as the wind in the sails of the Modi wave. Arguably, the media moved from 'manufacturing consent' to 'manufacturing dissent' against the UPA before it returned again to 'manufacturing consent' for Modi and his government.[33]

RIGHT-WING RESURGENCE

The fall of the Congress and Modi's arrival signals a shift of political landscape to the right. The 2014 election verdict was not simply a defeat of the Congress; it was also a defeat of various progressive forces which were unable to provide any coherent alternative. The BJP's coming to power is, therefore, not just one party replacing the other but an indication of a significant shift in the ideological discourse of Indian politics. Modi's decision to disband the Planning Commission has to be seen in this context. Abolishing the Planning Commission within three months of coming to power marked a clear break from the economic policy tradition that Jawaharlal Nehru and the Congress under his leadership represented. Though the Planning Commission faltered in its developmental role, the decision to scrap rather than reform it indicates a systematic dismantling of checks and balances. It indicates that the role of the state would be minimal with regard to social welfare, and there will be much stronger adherence to markets, business and entrepreneurship. Neo-liberal policies have gained momentum as the BJP seeks to undo many of the progressive measures introduced by the UPA government of the last decade. An emphatic rejection of the Congress legacy with regard to these policies is further evident from the 2015–16 budget which leans in favour of the corporates and taxpaying class at the expense of the poor. Reductions in allocations for Scheduled Castes and Scheduled Tribes and the Integrated Child Development Scheme (ICDS) can be cited as examples of the shift.

Modi's greatest success lies in his ability to refashion Hindu nationalism by adopting a developmentalist stance 'redefined as both aspirational and nationalist'.[34] The effort to dovetail religious nationalism with economic progress has led to a widespread belief that the BJP has gone beyond its communal agenda with its new emphasis on development and governance, when in fact 'development' and 'growth' have aligned with conservative social values and institutions to form the basis of right-wing resurgence in the country.[35] Very many people have bought into this rhetoric; indeed, many see it as India's best bet for getting ahead. A large section of the electorate is not bothered about majoritarianism as long as it does not affect their personal domain, and as long as the government succeeds in delivering higher economic growth and jobs. Significantly, this current of conservative ideology sits comfortably with education, prosperity and consumption.[36] It lacked electoral legitimacy previously but has gained wide acceptability, thanks to popular mobilization efforts of the Modi campaign which sought to justify it as an expression of the will of the majority.

The Congress's revival hinges on its ability to address its crisis of credibility, encouragement of state leaders, and functioning as a vigorous Opposition in Parliament, and outside. In the long road ahead, the Congress will have to rebuild itself as a credible alternative to Modi and the BJP which stand for both economic and social conservatism. Any attempt to reshape itself as pale saffron in a bid to mimic the winner will only help to legitimize the right-wing political discourse, while failing to pick up the electoral dividends from this competitive wooing of the Hindu vote. It is, therefore, essential that the Congress leads a nationwide campaign to counter and negate the long-term social and political impact of right-wing ideas and policies. A critique of and mobilization against the BJP's change of emphasis from the path of social welfare and communal harmony charted by the UPA over the last decade to majoritarian neo-liberalism should form the basis of its own political and organizational mobilization for revival and survival.[37]

However, without a dynamic leadership, voters will not look to the Congress as a viable political choice. The real key to rejuvenation lies in mass contact, the kind of platform that it adopts and the leadership's ability to communicate that to the people on the ground rather than the eternal verities of dynastic leadership.

NOTES

1   Jairam Ramesh, Interview by Supriya Sharma, *Scroll.in*, 24 February 2014, accessed on 24 February 2014.

2   Zoya Hasan, 'The Congress' moment of truth', *The Hindu*, 11 August 2014.

3   'Dark Decade in Governance: BJP's Chargesheet on Congress-led UPA', www.bjp.org/.../A%20Dark%20Decade%20in%20 Governance%20Aaro... accessed on 10 February 2015.

4   Economic Times Bureau, 'UPA presided over a wasted decade: BJP', *The Economic Times*, 19 January 2014.

5   Anil Padmanabhan, '2004 to 2014: India's lost decade', *Livemint*, 10 January 2014.

6   *Mint*, http://www.livemint.com/trading-up

7   Mihir Sharma, 'Farewell, a golden age', *Business Standard*, 11 May 2014.

8   Maitreesh Ghatak, Parikshit Ghosh and Ashok Kotwal, 'Growth in the time of UPA: Myths and Reality', *Economic and Political Weekly*, No. 16, 19 April 2014.

9   Ibid.

10 Jayati Ghosh, 'Change the Policy Mindset', *Tehelka*, 22 August 2013.

11 Mritiunjoy Mohanty, 'The growth model has come undone', *The Hindu*, 11 July 2012.

12 Kunal Sen, '"It's the economy, stupid": How the poor economic performance of the UPA regime is a key issue in the Indian elections', University of Nottingham Blogpost, 8 May 2014.

13 Pradeep Chhibber and Rahul Verma, 'The BJP's 2014 Modi Wave: An Ideological Consolidation of the Right', *Economic and Political Weekly*, Vol. XLIX, No. 39, 27 September 2014, p. 50.

14 Harish Khare, 'This perverse rage against the poor', *The Hindu*, 30 August 2013.

15 Jean Dreze and Amartya Sen, *An Uncertain Glory: India and Its Contradiction*, New York: Allen Lane, 2013, pp. 254–56.

16 Hartosh Singh Bal, 'Family Ties', *Caravan* Magazine, 1 January 2015.

17 'My mother came to my room and cried ... because she understands that power is poison,' Rahul Gandhi had said in a highly emotional speech after taking over as the vice-president in the Jaipur session of the AICC in January 2013. Reported in 'My mother cried, she understands power is poison: Rahul', *The Hindu*, 20 January 2013.

18 Harish Khare, 'Can Rahul be Reborn', *Open Magazine*, 13 June 2014.

19 NDTV anchor Barkha Dutt quoted in Sadanand Dhume, 'The Last Gandhi', *First Post*, 19 August 2014.

20 'Congress Zero', Editorial, *The Hindu*, 12 February 2015.

21 After his return from his fifty-day sabbatical in early 2015, Rahul Gandhi appears serious about shouldering greater responsibility in the party and assuming a leadership role. There is no doubt that his sustained campaign against the BJP government on several issues, especially the Land Acquisition Bill, has put the government on the back foot. It has helped the Congress occupy the Opposition space and put the NDA on the defensive. But he is yet to unveil a systematic long-term plan for reviving the party or rebuilding the party organization which is in a shambles.

22 'Rahul Gandhi pushes for middle path in development', *Sakal Times*, 21 December 2014.

23 'Rahul Gandhi breaks silence on Jayanthi's charges', *The Hindu*, 5 February 2015.

24 Zoya Hasan, 'Rahul Revivalism: Rahul Gandhi's elevation and the Congress's future', *Caravan*, 1 March 2013.

25 Sonia Gandhi set up at least three major committees to review and reorganize the party. All the committees recognized the lack of internal democracy as one of the reasons for the growing disillusionment with the organization, and recommended ending the practice of selecting Pradesh Congress Committee chiefs by nomination. But these reports were shelved, for fear of stirring up the pot too vigorously and upsetting the status quo. See more at: http://www.caravanmagazine.in/perspectives/rahul-revivalism#sthash.FBdp0anq.dpuf

26 A.K. Antony, Mukul Wasnik, R.C. Khuntia and Avinash Pandey were members of this committee. Previous to this one, two more committees were headed by A.K. Antony to look into various Congress debacles and had come to the same conclusion that top leadership was in no way responsible for Congress defeats.

27 'A.K. Antony committee blames UPA govt for poll rout, lets Rahul Gandhi get away', *Financial Express*, 17 August 2014.

28 'Rahul Gandhi not responsible for Congress defeat in Lok Sabha polls: A. K. Antony', *The Economic Times*, 15 August 2015.

29 'Sonia Gandhi, Rahul Gandhi offer to resign from Congress posts after defeat, party refuses', *The Economic Times*, 19 May 2014.

30 Analysis by Association for Democratic Reforms (ADR) and National Election Watch (NEW) found that BJP cornered about 69 per cent of total donations made to parties in 2013–14 even though the party was not in power at the Centre when it gained the most. Kumar Vikram, 'BJP coffers bulged with corporate cash in Financial Year 14', *Mail Today*, 25 February 2015.

31 Harish Khare, *How Modi Won it: Notes from the 2014 Election*, New Delhi: Hachette, 2015.

32 Cited in P. Sainath, 'Many waves, and a Media Tsunami', *NewsClick*, 21 May 2014.

33 Zoya Hasan, 'Manufacturing Dissent: The Media and the 2014 election', The Hindu Centre for Politics and Public Policy, 2 April 2014.

34 Arvind Rajagopal, 'The reinvention of Hindutva', *The Hindu*, 4 March 2015.

35 Varghese George, 'A Hindutva variant of neo-liberalism', *The Hindu*, 4 April 2014.

36 Santosh Desai, 'Hope and Dread: 2014 begins and ends with it', *The Times of India*, 28 December 2014.

37 On this see, Editorial, 'On the Verge of Extinction', *Economic and Political Weekly*, Vol. L, No. 8, 21 February 2015.

The Decline of the Left: A Casualty of Ideological Contradictions

V. Krishna Ananth

Dr V. Krishna Ananth, a fellow-traveller and sympathizer of the Left, teaches at the Department of History, Sikkim University, Gangtok.

With only ten MPs in the current Lok Sabha, the Left has been reduced to irrelevance in national politics. And the crisis is so deep that even in its biggest stronghold West Bengal, where the Left Front ruled for thirty-four long years, its very existence is under threat[1] after being devoured, first, by the Trinamool Congress (TMC); and now under pressure from the Bharatiya Janata Party (BJP) in the wake of Narendra Modi's ascent to prime ministership.

Ironically, the seeds of the CPI(M) and the Left's dramatic decline in the 2014 elections lay in the equally dramatic rise in its profile in the decades after 1989. The CPI(M), with its other Left partners, played a major role in propping up the National Front government headed by V.P. Singh in November 1989. (It was the first time that a general election threw up a hung Parliament in India's short history of parliamentary democracy.) The party's decision to shore up a non-

Congress government through outside support meant that the Left was forced into doing business with the BJP as well whose eighty-nine MPs were as critical for the survival of the V.P. Singh government as the Left's forty-five. That made the Left an indirect ally of the BJP.

The position the party took in 1989 marked a radical break with its line until then. Which was to keep its distance from the BJP, or its predecessor the Bharatiya Jana Sangh. This had been its stance since the socialist leader Ram Manohar Lohia devised his strategy of anti-Congressism which, in 1967, saw the Congress defeated in nine states and replaced by the Opposition-led Samyukta Vidhayak Dal (SVD) in Uttar Pradesh just a month after the elections. The CPI(M), notwithstanding its anti-Congress stand, stayed out of such formations that included the Bharatiya Jana Sangh, later renamed BJP.

The point is that the CPI(M) had, since its inception in 1964, emerged as the alternative to the Congress in at least two states – West Bengal and Kerala. Besides, it also made inroads into the small north-eastern state of Tripura where it became the ruling party a few years later and continues to remain so over successive elections till date. It may be stressed here that the formation of the CPI(M) after the split in the Communist Party of India in 1964 was a fallout of the debate within the undivided party over whom Jawaharlal Nehru's Congress represented in class terms. The section which believed that the Congress represented the interests of a national bourgeoisie and was, therefore, progressive, remained in the CPI, while those who held Nehru and the Congress as representing the interests of a bourgeois–landlord combine willing to compromise with monopoly capital walked out to form the CPI(M). The CPI(M) held on to an anti-Congress line even while refusing to join the anti-Congress front cobbled together by Lohia's Socialist Party that included the Bharatiya Jana Sangh.

This dilemma – whether to recognize the Congress as progressive – marked the CPI(M)'s existence for a decade after 1967. An unwavering anti-Congress line was of importance in the Left's traditional strongholds (Kerala and West Bengal), and it helped the CPI(M) emerge as the rallying point for the non-Congress governments in these states. It was also able to gather a substantial number of MPs in the Lok Sabha from the two states. The fact that the CPI(M) was not a force in the Hindi-speaking region made it easier for the party to stay away from anti-Congress formations there. In other words, anti-Congressism served the party well in its own citadels while at the same time enabling it to take a nuanced stand vis-à-vis non-Congress parties where the Left was not a force to reckon with.

The Marxist approach to political strategy is that while man makes history, he does not do that in circumstances of his choice, and instead, the stages are determined by the objective reality in which he is located. So, the CPI(M) could not have remained pro-Congress and yet grown in West Bengal, or in Kerala. It is also a fact that its cadres were hounded by the Congress in both these states. The party also never forgot that the first communist government in Kerala elected in 1957 under the leadership of E.M.S. Namboodiripad was not allowed to complete its term by Nehru's Congress government in New Delhi on the pretext of a breakdown of law and order in the state following a spate of anti-communist protests by vested interests affected by its legislations on education and land reforms. Nehru's government misused Article 356 of the Constitution to remove it in 1959. The CPI(M)'s formation five years later was rooted in its distrust of the Congress; and its anti-Congressism helped it grow as an independent voice of the Left. The CPI, on the other hand, was to pay a heavy price for keeping faith with the Congress. Its progressive decline since then can be traced to its pro-Congress line.[2] It lost its distinct identity in the political discourse and was reduced to playing second fiddle to the CPI(M).

The relevant point for the purposes of this essay is that while the CPI(M)'s tactics did help it, the party's line against backing non-Congress Opposition in the Hindi-speaking region because of Jana Sangh's presence foreclosed its expansion outside West Bengal and

Kerala. It also meant that the Left did not participate in the anti-Congress agitations in the early 1970s such as the Nav Nirman Andolan in Gujarat or Jayaprakash Narayan's Total Revolution campaign in Bihar and Uttar Pradesh popularly known as the JP movement. The CPI(M) neither supported the movement nor opposed it, while the CPI publicly opposed it and ended up in the Congress party's lap.

However, during the Emergency (1975–77), the CPI(M) gave up its neutral stance in order to fight Indira Gandhi's authoritarian regime and threw its lot behind anti-Congress forces that included the Jana Sangh. This led to a crisis in the party when its veteran leader P. Sundarayya resigned as general secretary[3] protesting his comrades' 'revisionist habits'. Sundarayya's quarrel was on two issues. One was that a certain section holding control over the trade union front – the Centre of Indian Trade Unions (CITU) did not cooperate with the party in launching campaigns. But, more importantly, he was concerned that it was cooperating with the Jana Sangh–backed anti-Congress groups. Sundarayya's disagreement, in particular, was with party leaders in West Bengal who regarded the Congress as the sole enemy. He refused to accept that the CPI(M) must strive to wrest power in the elections and was among the minority who believed that revolutionary upsurge was the only correct Marxist approach. The election of E.M.S. Namboodiripad as general secretary at the party's tenth congress at Jalandhar in April 1978 marked a substantial change in the party's line, and the shift was formalized at the party's Salkia plenum that year.[4]

Two important aspects of the line adopted at the Salkia plenum were that the CPI(M) would henceforth be a *mass revolutionary* party; and that the party would strive to expand in the Hindi-speaking region and elsewhere by entering into joint actions with the non-Congress Opposition parties there. In other words, the Sundarayya line was rejected wholesale.

It was clear that its experience in West Bengal and Kerala, where it had emerged as a powerful electoral force (the party managed to wrest power from the Congress in West Bengal in 1977, even while losing the election in Kerala), had led it to accept the parliamentary path as much as a revolutionary agenda rather than persist with the Sundarayya line. Its immediate effect was that the CPI(M) embraced the Janata Party which by then had captured public imagination across the nation. The party, however, did not jettison its position of not doing business with the Jana Sangh.[5] Its moment to strike came when a rift emerged in the Janata Party over the continuing RSS links of some of its senior leaders such as Atal Bihari Vajpayee and L.K. Advani. In what came to be known as the 'dual membership' issue, Madhu Limaye called for Vajpayee and Advani's removal from Prime Minister Morarji Desai's cabinet unless they severed their links with the RSS. The CPI(M) decided against continuing support to the Desai government. A truncated Janata Party could have remained in power, even after the exodus of its MPs to Charan Singh's Janata Party (Secular), if the Left with a combined strength of forty-eight MPs had continued its support. This, however, did not happen and the Janata Party government collapsed.

In 1989, exactly a decade after the CPI(M) refused to condone any arrangement with the Jana Sangh and pulled down the Desai government, the party lent its support to another non-Congress government, this time despite the fact that this government was also dependant on support from the BJP. The CPI(M)'s consistent anti-Congress line that was further reinforced during the Emergency could only get further reified as the Congress, under Indira Gandhi, became more undemocratic in the 1980s, moving away even further from its moorings, under Rajiv Gandhi. Its 1989 position – a break with its previous policy of treating BJP as untouchable – was a logical culmination of its increasingly hard line against the Congress.

The problem, however, is that the CPI(M) claims to be anchored in a certain ideological paradigm that is different from other bourgeois parties. Thus, it refused to fall for the temptations of office when, quite rightly, it turned down a historic opportunity in 1996 to head a non-Congress government at the centre. It did not allow Jyoti Basu to accept the Janata Dal's offer of prime ministership, a decision Basu was to call a 'historic blunder'.

Harkishan Singh Surjeet, who took over as the party's general secretary from Namboodiripad in January 1992, sought to implement the Salkia plenum line literally. Under him, the party had a rather laissez-faire approach to ideology. Surjeet was comfortable in the company of a leader like Mulayam Singh and his power broker, Amar Singh. Ditto Lalu Prasad Yadav, despite facing serious charges of corruption; and the DMK and the AIADMK in spite of them flirting with the Congress or the BJP.

This was also the phase of liberalization when the Nehruvian economic policy with its thrust on public sector shifted to privatization and market economy. The Left parties, even while protesting against the shift, failed to build a consistent resistance. Thus, the Left Front government in West Bengal ended up attempting to implement the new policy.[6] The party's argument was that state governments, under the constitutional scheme, were without powers when it came to policymaking in the economic realm. It was strange, then, that the party decided to run state governments even while knowing so well that the extent to which it could implement its own policies was limited; and, yet, it rejected an offer for its leader to become the prime minister for the same reason!

The point is that the Left, even after sustaining the United Front (between 1996 and 1998) and the United Progressive Alliance (between 2004 and 2008), ended up losing its electoral base. From as many as fifty-three MPs in 2004, the combined strength of the CPI and the CPI(M) fell to 20 in 2009, and 10 in 2014. And, in 2011, the Left lost power in West Bengal, where it had ruled since 1977, and also in Kerala.

Therefore, it is important to identify the cause for its decline in the immediate context as much as one should in the long term. Inasmuch as we argue that the crisis was rooted in the Salkia plenum and the compromise thereof (to gloss over the party's line with such un-Marxist phrases as *mass revolutionary* rather than declaring the parliamentary road as its line), and the resort to such rhetoric that the party will seek to expand in the Hindi-speaking region by joint action with bourgeois parties (rather than charting a course similar to Left parties in the West and participating in coalition governments), the CPI(M) ended up falling between two stools. Trade unions, the mainstay of any communist party, turned out to be the most problematic. Industrial centres like Mumbai and Kanpur, traditional Left bastions, gravitated towards the BJP: a development that the Left could not explain even while recognizing its harsh reality. The fact is that the Left unions did not go beyond wages and bargain; and it had serious implications for the Left's political future in the face of the twin challenge of corporate liberalization and the rise of Hindutva. The two, in fact, were not isolated events.[7]

The 1990s witnessed both these trends emerging in our political discourse, and with the BJP-led NDA coming to power in 1998, the Left swung to the other end of the spectrum: from anti-Congressism to anti-communalism. May 2004 marked this shift with the Left agreeing to extend support to the Congress-led UPA Government. The events after the Left's decision to withdraw its support to the UPA in 2008 and the splendid isolation it suffered as a result was only the culmination of the compromise at Salkia. The Left remained restricted to its traditional strongholds of West Bengal and Kerala while in Tamil Nadu, Andhra Pradesh and parts of Bihar, places where the movement had a strong presence historically, its base eroded substantially.

This is the context in which the Left Front government's approach to economic development in West Bengal became the immediate cause for what can be called its terminal decline. The Left Front in West Bengal, unlike in Kerala, appeared invincible. West Bengal was among the states where the Congress party had turned weaker than before in election after election since 1977. The Congress decline, in fact, had begun even earlier in West Bengal as in Tamil Nadu. It began with the reverses as far back as the 1967 elections and the crisis deepened in the 1990s.

But while the growth of the Left as an electoral force was coterminous with the decline of the Congress, the fact that this growth was restricted mostly to only three states – West Bengal, Tripura and Kerala – meant that the Left was only one of the many groups that replaced the Congress. Most of them, however, were organizationally weak; and this created a vacuum for the BJP and regional parties to step in.

The CPI(M), while setting its line at the Salkia plenum, even while aware of the possibility of such a risk, opted to gloss over it. The party's leaders, after all, were not naive to imagine that they could grow in Uttar Pradesh, Bihar and elsewhere in the country by striking electoral alliances with the non-Congress, non-BJP parties in these states. The fact is that the party charted its course in the reality in which it existed – an alternative to the Congress in West Bengal and Kerala, a marginal player in such states as Tamil Nadu and Andhra Pradesh and a mere paper organization elsewhere in the country. The trouble is that the leadership shied away from placing this understanding on record and, instead, pretended to hold on to Leninist notions of the state and revolution. Notwithstanding the fact that there is no mention whatsoever of a revolutionary transformation in the programme of either the CPI(M) or the CPI, the party's rank and file were convinced by its leaders that theirs was not just another political party; they were told, day after day, that the party's strategic goal was a socio-economic and political transformation. At the same time, the party used the Salkia line to pursue precisely the same policies which, otherwise, it derided as revisionist or reformist. This was taken to its height by Harkishan Singh Surjeet during the United Front rule (1996–98).

The Left's decision to withdraw support to the UPA on the issue of the Indo-US nuclear deal in 2008, widely held as the cause for its subsequent decline, should have been an opportunity for its leaders to introspect. It was an opportunity to think as to whether the party's strategic ends were compromised due to the Salkia line; and whether the party should opt for the parliamentary path and create spaces for strategic negotiations from within the parliamentary structure. (After all, the Left had worked within constitutional confines and carried out substantial agrarian reforms which made the system in West Bengal and Kerala more egalitarian than elsewhere in the country.) Instead, the party leaders chose to remain stuck in a time warp. This led to a gnawing gap between the party's precept and practice. And it was most pronounced in the way the government in West Bengal sought to implement some aspects of the market-oriented economic policy as illustrated by the manner in which farmland was acquired for Tata Motors to set up a car factory in Singur; and attempts to forcibly acquire land in Nandigram for establishing a Special Economic Zone (SEZ) to help exporters.

A generation of communists who built the party and its organization against a repressive regime came to be replaced by a managerial class of leftists. These time servers, who came to fill the party's ranks and its structures, contributed immensely to its alienation from its support base of small farmers and landless proletariat. Marxist scholars have established that the theory of democratic centralism, historically, has been reduced to a rule by party bosses. The CPI(M)'s party organization in West Bengal and Kerala is no exception to this. That is why it took so long for the party even to concede that it was wrong to use violence against farmers who resented their land being handed over to industrialists or seized for housing projects. Yet, the CPI(M) had opposed such moves in non-Left-ruled states.[8]

The intensity of the protest in West Bengal against such land acquisition was a way of Left's supporters asking it: 'Et tu Brutus?' They couldn't believe that a party, which had led movements against such tactics, was now doing this to them. And this made them more angry than they would have been if, say, the Congress had done a similar thing. It was a case of the Left's political and historical legacy coming to haunt it.

It was in 2006 that the Left Front government in West Bengal began to work in a concerted manner to develop the state on the lines proposed under the Central government's liberalization/privatization framework. The fact that the party cadre was found to have engaged in physical violence against farmers who resisted alienation of their farmlands meant that the Left had ceased to be Left. It suffered substantial losses in West Bengal to the benefit of Mamata Banerjee's Trinamool Congress. This should have been taken as a warning for the Left to introspect and correct its ways. The writing on the wall was clear. But the Left did not care to read it, and two years later the inevitable happened. It was thrown out in the 2011 elections to the state assembly.

It was a case of the party losing its support base – the small and middle peasant class and the minority community – in its quest for urban middle-class votes. In the rest of India, the party reduced itself to behaving like a ragpicker, desperate to collect anything it could lay its hands on. Thus, it attempted arrangements with the likes of YSR Congress, whose leader Jagan Mohan Reddy was known to have amassed riches when his father was chief minister of Andhra Pradesh; the AIADMK whose leader was known for using allies and then discarding them after they had served their purpose, and was to end up in jail after being convicted for corruption; and the Samajwadi Party which was to rescue the UPA government after the Left withdrew support. It was more interested in cobbling together a Third Front rather than attempting a course correction that could have saved the Left from the ignominy it suffered in May 2014.

The Left had a historic opportunity to reinvent itself and position itself as the platform of resistance against the fallout of the economic slowdown. It could try and capture the imagination of the middle classes as Anna Hazare and Aam Aadmi Party's anti-corruption campaign did. But the Left's own hands were none too clean when it came to corruption, given its record in states where it had ruled. The Left could have found common cause with protest movements on issues of environment, democratic and civil rights and good governance. But here too, its own record in West Bengal and Kerala had been controversial.

So, here's my brutal verdict on the current state of the Left: only a miracle can help it revive, and restore its relevance. But, miracles do happen in politics and it will be rash to write off the Left completely. After all, the Congress has had several revivals. So, all is not yet lost for the Left, but given the shambolic state of its organization, especially in West Bengal, it will take a lot of hard work and a new way of thinking for it to regain its relevance in national politics. The question is: does it have what it takes to perform a miracle?

NOTES

1 I should state here that the thrust of the arguments here is on the CPI(M) and its position. The CPI, though a separate party with its own programme and a distinct identity, has been on the decline over a period since the party split in 1964 and the formation of the CPI(M). In a sense, the decline of the CPI since the split was caused by the party's line to side with the Congress party; it must be noted that this is not the case, entirely, with the CPI(M). Similarly, we are not discussing the Forward Bloc and the Revolutionary Socialist Party, though they are part of the Left Front, in this essay for the reason that these parties have not asserted a distinct identity and have gone with the CPI(M) on all issues.

2 The number of CPI members in the Lok Sabha has been decreasing since 1977 (when it won twenty-three seats) and the party has just one MP in the sixteenth Lok Sabha.

3 P. Sundarayya was elected general secretary of the CPI(M) when the party was founded in 1964 and held that position until he resigned and E.M.S. Namboodiripad became the general secretary in 1978.

This was perhaps the only instance in the history of any communist party in India where the general secretary of the party resigned. A long note by Sundarayya to the members of the Central Committee of the CPI(M) was not known to the outside world until the late 1980s and is now a public document.

4 A plenum is a plenary session of a communist party from where a pronounced shift in the line is formalized. The Salkia plenum in 1978 was one such instance and the CPI(M) continues to be guided by the position adopted then.

5 It must be noted that though the Jana Sangh had merged into the Janata Party, it is a fact that the core elements of this platform maintained their distinct identity and they were concerted in their efforts to implement the RSS agenda making use of their positions in the Union cabinet as well as in the state governments that the Janata Party had captured in the June 1977 round of assembly elections.

6 The irony of the Left parties opposing the policy, even while pushing such projects as soft drink plants by Pepsico and Coca Cola (the two American multinational corporation [MNCs]) or making way for shopping malls in their own backyards, was not lost and the CPI(M) leaders simply brazened it out or responded with arguments of ridicule.

7 I have argued this elsewhere. See V. Krishna Ananth, 'Globalisation and Communalism: Locating the Contemporary Political Discourse in the Context of Liberalisation', in Ram Puniyani (ed.), *Religion, Power and Violence: Expression of Politics in Contemporary Times*, New Delhi: Sage, 2005.

8 I must add that the Left's opposition to such land grabs in Odisha, Uttar Pradesh or Andhra Pradesh were more by way of statements and there was hardly any mobilization of the people in such instances. It is also important to stress here that such resistance to the liberalization regime were built, since 1991, by the Maoists and such other non-parliamentary Left platforms.

Modi's World: Beyond Selfies and Tweets

Andrew Whitehead

Andrew Whitehead is a former BBC correspondent based in Delhi and was the editor of BBC World Service News until the spring of 2015. He is now an honorary professor at the Institute of Asia and Pacific Studies at Nottingham and visiting senior research fellow at the King's India Institute in London. He has a PhD in South Asian history and is the author of *A Mission in Kashmir*.

Selfies and social media posts are hardly the substance of Narendra Modi's engagement with the world, but they have certainly helped to set the tone. And much of his diplomacy in his first year at Racecourse Road has been about tone.

A week ahead of Modi's first visit as prime minister to China in May 2015, he set up an account on Sina Weibo, the hugely popular Chinese micro-blogging site which hosts more than 100 million posts a day. 'Hello China! Looking forward to interacting with Chinese friends through Weibo,' read his first, less than revelatory, post. But it was in

Chinese and aimed at the Chinese people – they noticed, and so too did the world's news media.

Once in Beijing, the Indian prime minister took a selfie outside the Temple of Heaven with China's premier Li Keqiang, a leader less accustomed to this form of digital narcissism. Modi promptly posted the image on Twitter – attracting lots of media and social media attention, including comment about how he had found a way through China's 'Great Firewall' which restricts access to the Internet. It is the defining image of his visit. And just to underline this, Vikas Swarup, the spokesperson of India's Ministry of External Affairs (better known as author of the novel that formed the basis of the movie *Slumdog Millionaire*), tweeted an image of his prime minister taking the photo, describing it as 'the ultimate selfie'. The *Wall Street Journal* went even further and mused about whether this was 'the most politically power-packed selfie in history'.[1]

Other leaders, among them Australia's Tony Abbott, have also featured in Modi's selfies. Unlikely as it may seem for a man in his sixties with no children, Modi has made more of social media than any of his peers around the world. It's a follow-on from one of the more adventurous aspects of an exceptionally successful BJP campaign in the 2014 general election. He emerged from that with more than four million followers on Twitter, and among the top tweets of the election was Modi's selfie with ink-stained finger after casting his vote. A special app allowed his supporters to have their own 'selfie with Modi'. In diplomacy as in politics, Modi has sought to portray himself with an informality and engagement which challenge the standard image of a senior Indian politician; in diplomacy as in politics, it is all very much about him.

There is something of the showman about Narendra Modi – he clearly enjoys the world stage, the performance and the applause, just as he relishes the campaign platform. In his first year in office, he has travelled relentlessly, restlessly almost. There have been eleven international trips in those twelve months, with eighteen nations visited, including the United States, Japan, Brazil, Germany, France and several of India's neighbours. The effort and political capital he has spent in diplomacy has surprised observers. No one expected him to put as much emphasis on India's place in the world as on economic reform back home.

Broadly, his visits have been successful – sometimes emphatically so. The combination of charm and steely-eyed purpose which won over the Indian electorate has served him well in the world's capitals. No other Indian prime minister outside the Nehru–Gandhi dynasty has achieved this level of visibility. It suits his personal, and personalized, style of leadership. Modi has been his own foreign minister, not in name (Sushma Swaraj holds the office) but certainly in fact. 'In the course of a long conversation he never once refers to any of his ministers ...' reported one of the few Western journalists to interview Modi.[2] 'When speaking about world affairs, he focuses on his personal rapport with other leaders. He seems to think he is the government.'

That's in part because Narendra Modi feels he has something to prove. When the *Economist* asked about his many foreign trips, he explained these were necessary to allow the 'international community to get an opportunity to assess me directly', pointing to a personal insecurity as well as a purpose. As recently as on 13 February 2014, the US ambassador to India called on Modi at his residence in Gandhinagar to draw a close to almost a decade of cold-shouldering the Gujarat chief minister. He had been denied a visa for the United States in 2005 under a law which restricts the entry of those seen as responsible for 'severe violations of religious freedom'.

Several other Western nations also placed Modi in diplomatic quarantine, though most were quicker off the mark than the US in lifting these restrictions when it was clear he was a strong prospect to become prime minister. By the time Nancy Powell turned up for her awkward hour-long meeting in Gujarat's capital city, the first day of voting in India's general elections was less than two months away. Such a late overture to the BJP's prime ministerial candidate was testimony to the depth of suspicion within at least sections of the US diplomatic community about Modi's perceived communalism and his culpability for the 2002 Gujarat riots.

Modi does not – by all accounts – 'forgive and forget', and the sense of wound at the way in which Western governments treated him is likely to linger still. But as a politician comfortable with power – how to wield it and how to accommodate it – he knew he had to brush over the traces of American censure. It was a personal priority. And he has enjoyed a resounding success. Within a year, he had both visited Barack Obama at the White House and hosted him as the chief guest at India's Republic Day ceremony. There seems to be a bond between the two leaders. In their political careers, both are after a fashion outsiders who have made it to the top – and for both, a sense of mission has been a foundation stone of their success.

Of all the accolades Narendra Modi has received in his first year, being named among *Time* magazine's 100 Leaders may not be in the top tier. But when that's accompanied by a personal encomium from the most powerful man in the world, now that really is something. Modi's 'life story from poverty to Prime Minister – reflects the dynamism and potential of India's rise', extolled Obama. 'Like India, he transcends the ancient and the modern – a devotee of yoga who connects with Indian citizens on Twitter and imagines a "digital India".'[3] Obama described his counterpart as 'India's reformer-in-chief'. Such a remarkable endorsement reflects an embrace both of India and its new leader. It would be difficult to think of a more demonstrable sign that Modi is welcome at the top table.

He was certainly lionized in New York, attracting 'a reception more befitting a rock star or a pope than a visiting foreign dignitary'.[4] In successive days, he appeared on stage in Central Park, where he was introduced by the actor Hugh Jackman between music acts at a Global

Citizen Festival, and filled Madison Square Garden for an extraordinary display of support from the affluent and successful Indian community in the US who have long been among his loudest supporters. This reflected two consistent aspects of Modi on tour: his desire to reach out directly to the host country and not simply through the more traditional means of speeches and news conferences, and his courting of the Indian diaspora who have sometimes felt unloved back home, regarded as in some way disloyal for making their lives away from the mother country and disbarred from full dual nationality. Modi seems determined to turn Indian communities worldwide into an agent of soft power, in much the way that yoga and Bollywood may be said to increase India's global profile.

OBAMA'S WARNING

Alongside the feel-good moments and the acclaim, there remains in Washington and other Western capitals an undercurrent of anxiety about the BJP's at times stridently assertive religion-based nationalism. If Barack Obama has delivered the choicest of tributes, he has also voiced anxieties about communal tension and violence in India. When he visited Delhi in January 2015, the US president pointedly told an audience of young Indians that their country 'will succeed so long as it is not splintered along the lines of religious faith'[5] – older Indians of course have lived through just such a splintering, the Partition that accompanied Independence in 1947. Obama returned to this theme of religious inclusivity a few days later at the annual National Prayer Breakfast in Washington when he brought into play the most famous of all Gujaratis, Mahatma Gandhi, perhaps as a veiled warning to a contemporary Gujarati: 'Michelle and I returned from India – an incredible, beautiful country, full of magnificent diversity – but a place where, in past years, religious faiths of all types have, on occasion, been targeted by other peoples of faith, simply due to their heritage and their beliefs – acts of intolerance that would have shocked Gandhiji, the person who helped to liberate that nation.'[6]

The concerns were couched as historic rather than current, but the lingering shadow of the violence in Gujarat early in Modi's time as chief minister is evident, as is an undertow of alarm about an authoritarian and majoritarian approach to governance.

This also found expression in untypically direct language from an ambassador – the new US ambassador to India, Richard Verma (whose parents were born in pre-Partition Punjab) – who expressed his concern about the tightening regulatory net around non-governmental organizations (NGOs) which receive funding from overseas, in which both Greenpeace and the Ford Foundation have become entangled. 'Because a vibrant civil society is so important to both of our democratic traditions,' Verma stated, 'I do worry about the potentially chilling effects of these regulatory steps focused on NGOs.'[7] He spoke of the importance of civil society in achieving advances in health care, economic inclusivity, environmental protection, human rights and the strengthening of democracy – a range of issues on which the BJP's record is at best patchy.

There are occasions when Modi's world view and social attitudes strike a discordant note with the modern, young, digital India he champions and seeks to represent. He is not by instinct a liberal. And there are moments when he, to use an Americanism, misspeaks. Early in his second year in office, Modi made his first visit to a Muslim-majority nation. He will have been surprised by the firestorm which greeted his clumsy compliment to his host, Bangladesh's Sheikh Hasina, praising her resolve in tackling terrorism 'despite being a woman'.[8] Almost instantly, #DespiteBeingaWoman started trending back home, with much comment about the unthinking chauvinism that Modi had imbibed from the RSS, the casual insult to Indian women, and the lack of historical awareness of Indira Gandhi's putting down of the Khalistan movement. It tarnished a visit meant to conclude and celebrate a landmark, a land border agreement between these neighbours which had taken forty years to iron out. Those who prosper by social media can also be humbled on those same platforms.

SUSPICIONS AND FEARS

Part of the difficulty Modi faces in winning friends around the world is the antediluvian reputation of Hindu nationalism. It is no longer tagged by an association with fascism, a simplistic description which is undeserved and profoundly misleading, but neither is it well understood in the West. During the only interruption in India's post-Independence, universal franchise democracy – the twenty-one months of Indira Gandhi's Emergency – BJP leaders were among those detained. The party's democratic credentials are strong. But there is a sense that it sees Hindus as more equal than others; that it is in significant measure controlled by the opaque and somewhat menacing RSS; that it sponsored the Ayodhya demolition in 1992 and so unleashed the ensuing carnage; and that some in its ranks may at times be willing to tolerate communal violence either to keep minorities in their place or because they don't know how to rein in more hard-line elements. This has damaged its standing around the world. Diplomats are well acquainted with Congress-led governments; the BJP in power is a lesser-known quantity, and still viewed with a fair measure of caution.

Modi's personal diplomacy is a response to that, and he and those around him have taken steps to try to mend any lingering perception that he is a communal hardliner who may have blood on his hands. One of his campaign team, a lawyer based in London, approached the political writer Lance Price, a former BBC correspondent who went on to work in Tony Blair's Downing Street (one wonders if Modi wanted a bit of the Blair stardust) and wrote a well-received account of his time there. Price was offered access to India's new prime minister. That's a rare commodity.

Modi does not often make himself available to the news media, and especially to English-language liberal-inclined networks and journalists. Price had four hour-long interviews with Modi. No restrictions were placed on what he could ask, and no copy approval was sought. But he appears to have been chosen in part because, in Price's words, he 'came with no prejudices or preconceptions'. He was not an expert on India and knew little initially about the row over Modi's handling of the 2002 riots and their aftermath. Price's book about Modi and the election campaign which made him prime minister is no whitewash, but it's nothing like as censorious of its subject as several other accounts.[9] Not that Modi agreed to talk directly about the riots. 'I have said enough,' he told Price, 'and you can read the reports and the Supreme Court judgment for yourself.' The book concludes that Modi can be confident that he will be judged henceforward 'on what he achieved in office and no longer on events in the past'.

This rubbing out of the blot of the 2002 riots is what Modi wants. The consensus in Western corridors of power appears to be that whatever the unease about Modi's conduct as chief minister at that time, it is indeed necessary to move on. The much expressed concern about his alleged culpability may make him determined to avoid any further communal violence on his watch. And an Indian leader who wants to strike a new, more positive note in his country's engagement with Western powers needs to be met halfway. Narendra Modi has got off to a good start, and those major countries that didn't host him in his first year are anxious to do so. But to build on the buzz that he has undoubtedly created, there needs to be more substance to his diplomacy. The biggest game changer in India's foreign policy in recent years has been the civil nuclear deal with the US which Manmohan Singh's government saw through, not anything that Modi has achieved. He needs something to blog about which merits more than 140 characters.

NOTES

1 *Wall Street Journal*, 15 May 2015, http://blogs.wsj.com/indiarealtime/2015/05/15/did-modi-just-take-the-most-powerful-selfie-in-history/, accessed on 11 June 2015. For a study of 'twiplomacy', see http://twiplomacy.com/blog/twiplomacy-study-2014-update/, accessed on 11 June 2015.

2 *Economist*, 23 May 2015, http://www.economist.com/news/special-report/21651325-indias-leader-needs-offer-vision-what-he-wants-achieve-and-let-others-help, accessed on 8 June 2015.

3 *Time*, 16 April 2015, http://time.com/3823155/narendra-modi-2015-time-100/, accessed on 1 June 2015.

4 *Washington Post*, 26 September 2014, http://www.washingtonpost.com/world/asia_pacific/indias-modi-begins-rock-star-like-us-tour/2014/09/26/eeabe78b-9327-4643-a131-33ab5c59174a_story.html, accessed on 8 June 2015.

5 https://www.whitehouse.gov/the-press-office/2015/01/27/remarks-president-obama-address-people-india, accessed on 11 June 2015.

6 https://www.whitehouse.gov/the-press-office/2015/02/05/remarks-president-national-prayer-breakfast, accessed on 11 June 2015.

7 *Hindustan Times*, 7 May 2015, http://www.hindustantimes.com/india-news/us-warns-of-chilling-effect-of-india-s-ngo-crackdown/article1-1344555.aspx, accessed on 11 June 2015.

8 *Times of India*, 8 June 2015, http://timesofindia.indiatimes.com/tech/social/DespiteBeingAWoman-PM-Modi-faces-flak-for-sexist-comment/articleshow/47583012.cms, accessed on 11 June 2015.

9 Lance Price, *The Modi Effect: Inside Narendra Modi's Campaign to Transform India*, London: Hodder & Stoughton, 2015.

The Media: Moving to the Right?

Sevanti Ninan

Sevanti Ninan writes on the media and is the founder editor of the media watch website thehoot.org.

The catch-all label of 'media' is increasingly used to describe a technologically diverse universe of communication. To this, we ascribe a common behaviour pattern. As in, the media is turning right, or turning saffron, or enabling the ascent of Narendra Modi. But is there a pattern, and is it consistent?

The sheer size of the beast called media – the thousands of publications, hundreds of channels and a multitude of new media users participating in the public sphere – has led to the notion that the media is an actor.

When in May 2014 the Bharatiya Janata Party (BJP) won a decisive mandate to rule the country, commentators suggested the media had played a role. The sheer amplification of the prime ministerial contender's campaign, much of which was technological, contributed to this impression. But May 2014 (and a series of other state elections victories that year) was followed by the Delhi Legislative Assembly elections in February 2015. A mighty win followed by a mighty loss. Where did television, newspapers, Internet and radio figure as influencers? If they were thought to have created the climate for a big victory, how did that effect dissipate in barely nine months?

Ten days after the elections to the Delhi Legislative Assembly the prime minister, thought to be chastened by his party's ignominious defeat (a mere three seats for the BJP in a seventy-seat assembly) made a speech at a Christian forum asserting that freedom of religion would be protected at all costs. A host of newspaper editorials, foremost among them the right-wing *Dainik Jagran*, roundly criticized his delay in speaking up after several incidents of physical attacks on churches and minority-baiting by both his ministers as well as Hindutva groups in the preceding months had gone unchallenged. In an editorial titled '*Sahi Sandesh Mein Deri*' (Delay in giving the right message) the paper said he should have spoken up unequivocally much earlier, and had he done so the actions of fringe Hindutva groups might not have cost his party the Delhi election. Secularism, added the *Hindustan Times* tartly, is a constitutional principle, not a policy option.

So can the media be accused of jettisoning liberal values?

If it is collectively believed to be an actor in the current Indian polity, we need to step back and understand the shifts taking place in its role as an influencer. Three distinct strands have come together to create an enabling media environment for a twenty-first-century, right-wing polity.

First, two decades of liberalization have led to a huge expansion of advertising-supported media, and shaped the economic philosophy of a new generation of media owners and editors.

The second strand is the rapid growth of the Hindi media, which is at once an amalgam of cultural conservatism and rising consumerism.

And third, the growing influence of new media on an increasingly cyber-savvy middle class, an influence whose potential Modi was alive to long before other politicians. For reasons yet to be sufficiently researched, right-wing opinion dominates this media.

LEAVE IT TO THE MARKET

Economics more than politics is the lens through which post-liberalization media views India's problems. The first strand in creating the climate for a right-wing polity to prevail is the growing conviction in sections of the mainstream media about more market-based solutions to eradicating poverty.

In August 2014, Raghav Bahl, the founder of Network 18 who had a few months earlier sold his stake in the company to Reliance Industries, spelt out his definition of liberalism: 'If more than three decades of state effort have not lifted people out of poverty, perhaps, it is best to trust them to get out of it themselves. For that, we need a state that will not get in their way as they try to get on with life. The motive force of liberalism is individual initiative. This presupposes personal liberties, the rule of law and an enabling state ... Liberalism is a sensibility, not an ideology.'[1]

He added, 'Most political outfits across the country are left-of-centre believers in a strong, meddling state. They may be pro-business, but not necessarily pro-market. When in power, they frame the terms of engagement in such a way that discretion is the rule, not the exception.'

He asked, 'Is advocacy of a right-liberal policy shift an invitation for a crony-capitalist takeover?' And went on to give examples of the crony capitalism which marked the tenure of United Progressive Alliance (UPA) whose government the BJP had replaced a few months earlier.

Bahl was an influential media owner. He owned majority stake in a business which ran the country's leading business news channel as well as two other channels, a magazine, *Forbes India*, and an Internet news portal called *First Post*, until his business was taken over by Reliance in 2014. Thereafter, he remained a non-executive director in Network 18. His personal conviction in the run-up to the 2014 elections was that the poor were not getting anywhere under a regime which professed a rights-based approach to uplifting those at the bottom of the heap.

He backed Modi's candidacy, and wrote after the elections, 'Among the current political leaders, Prime Minister Narendra Modi has been an evangelist of private initiative. In his election speeches, he has been urging the youth to aspire to be job creators and not job seekers.'

In assessing liberalization's role in loosening the left-liberal hold on the media of opinion, one cannot underestimate the genuine conviction that a post-Independence generation of both media owners and editors brought to their advocacy of more market-based solutions to the country's problems. Many of them owned or worked for the business press which saw such major expansion in the decades after liberalization that India boasts of more business dailies (five in English and two in Hindi) than far bigger economies. In addition, there are six business news channels, including two in Hindi.

The economy rivals politics as a source of news for the non-business press as well. And the media as a whole, with very few exceptions, judges governments today primarily on their performance on economic growth and reforms. The latter is a catch-all word for labour reform, increasing privatization of the pubic sector, and the opening up of more sectors of the economy to foreign direct investment, including infrastructure.

Like Raghav Bahl, Shekhar Gupta, who was the high-profile editor of *The Indian Express* for two decades until he exited last year, also articulated his conviction on the irrelevance of left-liberalism for India's current challenges. During his stewardship, the paper was staunchly for economic reform. In Gupta's view, the Congress, immediately after independence, was a political umbrella wide enough to give room to liberals of the Left as well as the Right, but between them Jawaharlal Nehru and Indira Gandhi made social liberalism a Left monopoly, and pushed the Right into the arms of saffron elements.

'I am not sure Dr Manmohan Singh quite looked at it this way, but post-1991, he was probably the only famous liberal of old who thought it was time to delete the hyphenated left. By the middle of

2009, with a bigger second mandate, he was winning this campaign of ideological correction. But he was defeated by the party's embedded pinko immune system.'[2]

The elitism of the left-liberal in his view had denied opportunity to a rising mass of aspirational Indians until economic reform created precisely that: more opportunity for those who had not got it by virtue of birth. Implicit in the philosophy expounded by Bahl, Gupta and others is the belief that the poor need opportunities rather than rights.

The dominant narrative in the mainstream media, post-liberalization, has been one of advocating growth and economic reform as the path to poverty removal. The left-liberal critique of how the media, as an agenda setter, has pushed the values of the economic Right is articulated by Zoya Hasan in her essay 'Manufacturing Dissent: The Media and the 2014 Indian Election', published by the *Hindu* Centre for Politics and Public Policy. In examining the role of the media in framing issues before the country, she says it was the overwhelmingly privately owned media and TV channels in particular which helped to paint the Congress as 'corrupt, dynastic, and inefficient and a reckless benefactor of the poor'.

According to Hasan, the media as a platform promoted a political discourse which reflected middle-class anger at the economic slowdown, and attacked rights-based welfare schemes as 'doleconomics' and irresponsible populism which would destroy the growth story. She also contends that the achievements of the UPA government in bringing about some reduction in poverty were not given due credit in the coverage preceding elections. Moreover, 'there was an unprecedented attack on the National Food Security Act, as an instance of irresponsible populism that will destroy the growth story forever'.

The privately owned media could have made the riposte that since it was the same Congress party which had brought in economic reform in an earlier decade, it was hardly unreasonable to expect it to move the economy away from a need for doles, after two terms in power.

TELEVISION AND THE RIGHT

The birth and growth of the satellite and cable television industry in India coincided with the advent of liberalization in 1991. The growing availability of multinational advertising in its wake enabled media expansion. The double-digit growth of advertising which India was to see until the slowdown of 2008 has meant a giddy expansion in TV channels because the satellite transponder industry also took off around the same time. Which other country in the world has spawned 800-plus television channels? And managed to sustain them largely with advertising?

The expansion of print media too was fuelled by consumerism triggered by economic liberalization. If both motorcycles and Coca-Cola were to sell beyond district towns and find a market in the rural hinterland, a vehicle for advertising was needed. Thus was born, in the mid-1990s, the phenomenon of multi-edition Hindi newspapers, with an edition for every district. The south had led the way in the previous decade when *Eenadu* in Andhra Pradesh localized.

The 1990s saw the emergence of right-wing media entrepreneurs whose empires have grown. In 1992, Subhash Chandra, then a rice trader and entertainment park owner, hired a transponder and started Zee TV which grew over two decades into a multi-crore empire, part of the Essel Group. More to the point, Chandra has never hidden his allegiance to the BJP, even aspiring to a party ticket in the Haryana state elections in 2014. When he did not get one, he campaigned for the BJP candidate in the Hissar constituency. His news channels have played their part in building up Modi before and after his ascent to prime ministership.

Another media house that leans politically to the Right and has grown steadily more influential is the satellite channel called India TV. Headed by Rajat Sharma, a one-time student activist of the Akhil Bharatiya Vidyarthi Parishad (ABVP), the students' wing of the Rashtriya Swayamsevak Sangh (RSS), it has attracted investments from major corporations and was instrumental in providing a platform to the BJP's prime ministerial candidate in the run-up to the 2014 elections. Modi publicly acknowledged the debt when he spoke on the anniversary of Sharma's flagship talk show, *Aap ki Adalat*, in December 2014.

The structure of prime-time TV news in India has contributed, in no mean measure, to the BJP's consistent visibility in the years that it was out of power. In a low-cost news-manufacturing model where news gathering gives way to studio debate at prime time, the Opposition party, which has over the years built up a cadre of aggressive and articulate spokespersons, gets equal time with the one in power, with the anchor acting more as a referee in a slugfest. The more polarized the debate can be made, the more 'eyeballs' it is assured in a flawed television ratings system which is now being overhauled.

At election time, in particular, media becomes the site where the political process is played out. Elections are a godsend for both, the political candidate who needs to reach the voter, and a very large number of twenty-four-hour news channels looking for saleable news to fill airtime. Talk-based news meets the need of candidates looking for a platform. In the studios of Times Now, or NDTV 24×7 or Zee Business, the secular vs Hindutva debates or the ones on freebies versus responsible economics played out for several months in the build-up to the 2014 Lok Sabha elections as substitutes for genuine reporting from the ground.

But noise and optics should not be confused with substance.

Those actually in power don't let themselves be held to account by the news media. Ministers never have to come to a TV studio themselves, the prime minister rarely holds a press conference. In the UPA's ten-year tenure, Prime Minister Manmohan Singh held barely three press conferences. Modi, in the course of his long campaign to become prime minister, held none. Therefore, answering questions on the issues of the day has turned into an aggressive public relations exercise through spokespersons who are essentially PR men and women of political parties.

In the 2014 elections, both principal actors shunned the platform. Modi opted for rallies, and chose to take his message to the people without the mediation of a television anchor. Rahul Gandhi, the face of the Congress campaign, seconded deputies to fight the battle for him on television.

COVERING MODI

The irony of a personality-focused news culture (visible in the way the Delhi Legislative Assembly elections at the beginning of 2015 were covered, as in the Modi campaign of 2013 and 2014), is that political personalities deemed newsworthy are covered to the exclusion of all others; and the media ends up underwriting the poll expenses of some by giving free-of-cost exposure, while blacking out others who have no right to time in a ratings-driven news culture. No presumed demand, no coverage. And demand is presumed entirely on conjecture.

When measured by the Centre for Media Studies, it was found that in television's prime-time coverage in the run-up to the 2014 elections, Modi got significantly more airtime than Rahul Gandhi and Arvind Kejriwal. The channels devoted 33 per cent of their time to Modi, about 10 per cent to Kejriwal, and only about 4 per cent for Gandhi. In the final phase of elections, it went up to 40 per cent for Modi.

Did the media then cover Modi because it believed there was what you might call a box-office demand for him from news consumers? Or did it do so quite simply because he was making news by the sheer volume of his campaigning? Or was it because the mainstream media bought into the narrative that the country needed a decisive leader, and it was its job to do its bit to bring about that change?

All three were probably true. One should not however assume that all of the airtime was positive. As a Cleveland University academic

Anup Kumar has pointed out, 'We cannot ignore the context of the prime-time TV coverage. A large segment of the Modi-centric airtime was dominated by criticism of Modi and discussion of a genuine fear among minorities. The BJP tried to shift the debate away from secularism-communalism debate to governance-development debate in the prime-time news media, but failed.'[3]

There was also the issue of political advertising and what it was able to achieve. The BJP in the course of this election did a fair amount of advertising, particularly in the run-up to voting day in each part of the country, raising considerably the visibility of the candidate who had an edge in this contest. Modi was the face of the campaign. *'Ab ki baar Modi Sarkar'* (this time vote for a Modi government). The marketing was personality-centric, not party-centric. But then the party did the same for the February 2015 election and failed to carry the vote.

The fact that advertising seems to work in some elections but not in others suggests that it works only when things are going well for the party on the ground and the electorate is receptive.

NEW MEDIA QUEERS PITCH

New media increasingly influences the agenda for old media. It has also served to shrink the public sphere to those classes which are able to express themselves on the Internet. And when television channels take their vox populi feedback from what is trending on Twitter or Facebook rather than from what the street is saying, the dominance of the cyber-savvy over public discourse is complete. Particularly when they have an agenda and a mastery over the tools.

Even more than the BJP itself, Modi sought to shape the national discourse through his mastery of cyber politics. He used it to reach the segment he wanted to appeal to, newly enfranchised youth in the middle-class and neo-middle-class strata. He did Google hangouts, used Facebook, Twitter and YouTube, and he started early.

By 5 July 2013 he had become the most 'followed' politician on Twitter and the most liked Indian leader on Facebook. From May 2013, all his speeches were being telecast live on the Internet on YuvaiTV, and could be heard on telephones through a live audio bridge for a nominal fee. By January 2014 there was a downloadable caller tune and in February the *chai pe charcha*s began.[4] The media was captivated by the use of technology, particularly by the holograms which were an unprecedented gimmick in Indian election campaigning. The contrast with the face of the Congress campaign, Rahul Gandhi, who chose not to even be on Twitter, was one which worked well for Modi.

But the technology was far from ideology-neutral. The significance of the new media for the ascent of the BJP and Modi in 2013–14 was the anti-corruption, anti-dynastic, pro-Hindutva evangelism that a steadily growing volunteer force brought to the Modi campaign. A force of middle- and upper-middle-class techies, professionals and others whose numbers, vigour and vitriol gave rise to the term 'Internet Hindus'. They paved the way as much as they could for the man they wanted to see elected.[5]

But, given how fervent Internet denizens are about anti-corruption politics, you could argue that one reason February 2015 was different was perhaps because the Aam Aadmi Party, unlike the Congress, was able to tap the support of the cyber community as well.

A CHANGING DISCOURSE

Over two decades then, consistent left-liberalism in mainstream media – print and television – has become a minority stance which can be identified with specific publications: *The Hindu*, among the big mainstream newspapers; *Jansatta*, the Hindi publication of the *Indian Express* group; *Frontline*, from the *Hindu* stable; *Tehelka*, a stand-alone weekly. And specific TV channels, notably NDTV 24×7 and NDTV India.

But does that mean that the rest do not champion secularism, or bat for growth at the cost of displacement and environmental degradation, to take perhaps the single most contentious development issue in recent years? That has not been the case.

There are two issues that need to be separated in the view of media people who would describe themselves as belonging, in the twenty-first century, to the liberal Right: the issue of subscribing to Hindu majoritarianism, and the issue of which economic path to choose for a country where decades of left-liberalism has not succeeded in erasing poverty.

Shekhar Gupta, for one, has described the mainstream media as one of the intrinsically secular institutions in this country, like the Supreme Court, the Union Public Service Commission and the armed forces. And, indeed, it is the mainstream media that Modi shunned in his ascent to prime ministership, believing it to have stigmatized him for the Gujarat 2002 anti-Muslim riots long after he was cleared by inquiry commissions and courts.

In Uttar Pradesh, *Dainik Jagran* began to expand its district editions from the mid-1990s. The Kanpur-based Gupta family was headed by Narendra Mohan, who was for some time a BJP member of the Rajya Sabha. Over the subsequent two decades of expansion, the paper grew to acquire the highest readership in the country, alternating some years for number one position in readership surveys with the *Dainik Bhaskar*. In some situations of communal strife, *Jagran*'s role has been found to be suspect – in Ayodhya, in 1992, and more recently in Muzaffarnagar in 2013. Yet, as the *Jagran* editorial stance cited at the beginning of this chapter suggests, even this newspaper thinks jettisoning secularism would be dangerous politics for a ruling party.

As for the development discourse, in much of the mediascape it is still left to individual journalists to do incisive reporting on how enabling policy is translating on the ground, and affecting the economically marginalized. How you report environmental issues is a key indicator.

Corporate-owned or media-corporate-owned publications such as *The Times of India, Business Standard*, and *The Indian Express* have all done, over the past four years or so, sharp reporting on the subject, keeping a vigilant eye on environmental compromises both the UPA government and the NDA government were making to attract foreign investment.

Yet, the discourse has shifted unmistakably. As Malavika Sanghvi pointed out perceptively, villains and saviours seem to be getting reversed in the new India.[6] And the media has bought into this narrative. In the coverage surrounding the Greenpeace episode in January 2015, where an activist was stopped from going to testify before British parliamentarians about how Vedanta's mining is affecting tribals, NGOs are increasingly portrayed as obstructionists, whereas capitalists are the ones who will bring growth and jobs, provided obstacles are removed from their path. Gone are the days when the businessmen were the bad guys and the NGOs samaj sevaks, who served society. Investors are the new saviours.

Increasingly, media ownership has also begun to play a role in determining the stance a media outlet takes on issues such as land acquisition for mining, or the pricing of natural gas where the exploration is being done by the private sector. Corporate-owned media has to factor in corporate interests. Let me give just two examples. One of the two largest Hindi newspaper groups in the country, *Dainik Bhaskar*, is owned by a business group that also has interests in power and coal mining. Its editions in Chhattisgarh have to battle a conflict of interest while reporting on public hearings regarding land acquisitions where the company acquiring the land is also owned by their parent company. Will they be free to bat on the side of those who do not want their land taken over for captive coal mines?

And, after Reliance Industries acquired Network 18, those running its news channels have had to temper their coverage of a variety of issues: the accusations made by the Aam Aadmi Party in early 2014 about alleged favours done to Reliance in the pricing of natural gas, the recent revelations about alleged corporate espionage in the oil ministry by this industrial group, revelations about its banking deals in deference to the interests of the channel's ownership. Corporate self-censorship is increasingly in evidence.

So, is the media turning Right? Influential voices within it are. Is it losing its secular moorings? Influential voices within it are not. Are liberal concerns being rapidly jettisoned? Not yet. Even the Right wants to be able to describe itself as liberal.

NOTES

1 *Forbes magazine*, 8 August 2014.

2 'Saving Indian Liberalism from Its Left-Liberal Elite', *India Today*, 5 December 2014.

3 'A Media Role in Modi's Success?', 13 May 2014, thehoot.org.

4 Unpublished research paper, Meenal Thakur, 2014.

5 *India Today*, 'The Rise of the Cyber Hindu', 1 November 2013.

6 'North Versus the Rest', *Business Standard*, 31 January 2015.

An Aam NRI's View of the 'New' India

Rashmee Roshan Lall

Rashmee Roshan Lall is a journalist who has lived and worked in seven countries in the past eight years. She is the author of *The Pomegranate Peace*, a fictionalized account of the absurdity of American efforts in Afghanistan.

This is the ordinary NRI's guide to accepting that distance equals disenfranchisement, but dharma means if you see something, say something.

It is politic to start by acknowledging that many of my fellow Indians at home will dismiss this essay out of hand. To them, a non-resident Indian is no longer an authentic voice and consequently supremely unentitled to critique the motherland.

Never mind the tax status, the annual Pravasi Bharatiya Divas or the lifelong visa conferred by the Overseas Citizen of India card, the NRI loses leverage with every successive latitude and longitude of the journey away from home (22 degrees north of the equator, 78 degrees east of the prime meridian). Residence confers rights that are theoretically absolute as part of one's genetic inheritance.[1] Non-residence strips us of them. (Unless you follow the approved script, but we'll come to that later.)

By that token, I have almost no right to cast a critical eye or, god forbid, to find fault with the land of my fathers. I haven't lived there for any substantial length of time for twenty years, except for a brief period (2008 to 11) when I was editor of *The Sunday Times of India*. So, I have no rights. But, surely I can claim some civic responsibility, some sense of good citizenship of the world, of which 2.4 per cent of the land is occupied by India and in which one in every seven people is Indian.

Physical distance imparts a certain clarity to the way myopic people see faraway things. It's the same with the country of your birth, whose rough-diamond shape you first learnt to draw in class one. Today, with two passports, neither of which is Indian (how can they be, we still don't have dual nationality) it is still *'Jana Gana Mana'* that I can sing in my sleep, without thinking.

'We don't see things as they are, we see them as we are,' Anais Nin once said. She didn't mean the contortions – of perspective – necessary for those of us with absurdly over-hyphenated identities (I, for instance, am an American British Indian who has lived in four of the seven continents) though she might have done, being pretty hyphenated herself. She was born to Cuban parents in France, where she was raised; lived for a while in Spain and Cuba and most of her life in the US. But she didn't seem too troubled by that and more by the complications she introduced in her life as a consummate liar and bigamist. Her biographer, Deirdre Bair, says the writer dealt with her simultaneous marriages using something that she called the lie box.[2] Two sets of cheque books, made out in two different married names. Ditto, prescription bottles from doctors on the east coast of America and on the west. And she had a collection of file cards to write down the disparate lies just so she could keep them straight.

Like all serious philanderers, NRIs keep file cards too, mental ones at any rate, along with their 'India clothes', Indian mobile SIM cards and handy phone numbers of taxi drivers you can rely on to pick you up at the airport. The cards help remember the limits of candour – what is permissible to note as different, what is better left unremarked and the seemly levels of expressible exasperation at interminable paperwork, processes that don't work (along with government officials and large money transfers overseas), and too many demands for chai-pani.

But let us do without the file cards for once. 'Do you even recognize India now?' someone asked during discussion of this aam NRI's view of the 'new' India. To which the answer has to be: 'Yes, with joy and thankfulness and yes, with sadness and a dull shame.' India remains my country (with or without the passport), incredible and incredibly infuriating, the only place on the planet that I could turn up tomorrow and start to live without needing to find my feet and struggling to find my way. Yes, it has ATMs and malls and multiplexes now, and smart stores and cafes that are on trend with those dinky cupcakes and flat white coffees, but the internal logic of life remains just as it always was.

We remain large-hearted and hospitable and prone to strike up intimate conversations with rank strangers on buses and trains and planes. We still use the English language with a rapid fluency and a vocabulary and grammar that is pretty much only our own. We are still aware of spiritual concepts like karma, dharma and maya in a way that draws the world's admiration. We still value family and home cooking and, for better or worse, our good girls are still the ones who know the parameters of how to behave. We still pay the help only just enough to keep them at the job and still prefer the sweeper not to step into the kitchen. We still think more readily in terms of shame rather than guilt, which is to say the fear of being caught out rather than the actual wrong of doing something bad. The 'what will people say' school still wins.

So far, so general. The specifics of the changes are more troubling. Perhaps they can be best summed up in one relatively inexpensive product: the Gandhi mug. Nothing wrong with merchandizing; and that has its place – in the shops and in a tourism strategy. But the mug and the pillow covers and the other products bearing the face of Bapu,

Father of the Nation, say something about the new India that goes beyond any high-minded objection to crass commercialization.

It shows that we have become pragmatic in the extreme but probably still not practical enough to pass the Prince Philip test of sophisticated electrical work.[3] This pragmatism, the whatever-works-is-good philosophy, underscores a surrendering of faith in ourselves, in our essential goodness, in the need to live up to that ideal of goodness, the Gandhian template of striving to be as good as we can. We have lost our good will, that indispensable condition as Immanuel Kant described it, which can never be qualified. It just is. Intelligence or wealth, for example, or other gifts of fortune – power, honour can be considered bad in bad people. And good, if they are in good people. They derive their goodness from something other than their inherent quality. They can be qualified. But, 'a good will is not good because of what it effects or accomplishes, because of its fitness to attain some proposed end, but only because of its volition, that is, it is good in itself,' Kant said.[4]

It is possible to clearly discern the shift down the arches of the years as a long-gone NRI, but the contours of the coming change were becoming apparent even before I left. That Narendra Modi, supremely pragmatic and strikingly unremorseful about the deaths, on his watch, of thousands of Muslims in the 2002 Gujarat riots, is at the helm of a new India is a consequence of the change. He is not the reason for it.

ADVANI'S RATHYATRA

It is rare to be able to set a date for the transformation of a whole country and its mindset. But as a then-resident Indian journalist, I believe it really did kickoff on 25 September 1990, when L.K. Advani, then leader of Mr Modi's Bharatiya Janata Party (BJP), began his Ram rathyatra to Ayodhya to build support for the movement to reclaim the disputed Babri mosque for Hindus. The goal was to erect a temple dedicated to the infant Lord Ram, Ramlalla, at the site that the cultural nationalists believed to be his place of birth. A mosque, built in the

1520s on the orders of Babur, India's first Mughal emperor, stood on the site when Mr Advani set off from Somnath on the western coast, in a Toyota cannily redesigned as a rath, a traditional chariot.

The BJP's explanation[5] of the symbolism of the point of departure and the significance of the journey remains simple and stark, twenty-five years on: 'It was at Somnath that the assault on Hindu temples and shrines, the living symbols of an ancient nation, by Islamic invaders began – in 1026 the Somnath shrine was ransacked and its riches plundered by Mahmud Ghaznavi. The temple was rebuilt, only to be put to the sword again, and again, and yet again. But not all the armies of the invaders could kill the spirit of Somnath. In 1950, the destroyed temple was rebuilt at the initiative of Sardar Patel as a symbol of resurgent Indian nationhood. Shri Advani chose Somnath as the starting point of his yatra because the reconstruction of the shrine on the rubble of loot and plunder was the first chapter in a journey to "preserve the old symbols of unity, communal amity and cultural oneness".'

The idea of a chariot worked as 'a great mobiliser', *India Today* magazine reported at the time.[6] As a symbol, it illustrated the road worthiness of an ancient Hindu means of transport. It stoked an unsuspected 'can do' spirit, invoked Hindu pride and played upon barely buried competitive antagonisms.

Undivided India's Muslims, so the grouse went, had managed a two-stroke victory when Independence came around in August 1947 – they got a separate Muslim state, Pakistan, and those who stayed back in India got to be equal partners in the newly independent, staunchly secular state. Meanwhile, independent India's majority Hindu community got no more than the responsibility of maintaining good behaviour even as their Muslim fellow citizens repeatedly failed the so-called cricket loyalty test of patriotic allegiance during matches against Pakistan.[7]

That 1990 rathyatra, the first of many charged take-back-our-country initiatives by the Hindu nationalists, resulted in communal riots in

Gujarat, Maharashtra, Karnataka, Uttar Pradesh and Andhra. It also ended in the Babri mosque being torn down by a 200,000-strong mob. I was with *The Times of India* at the time and I still remember the agony of my disbelief as I watched BBC footage of the frenzy with which they used hammers to knock down the three domes and then tore at the bricks with their bare hands until the building was razed to the ground. From then, a new narrative became possible because the impossible had already happened. We could stamp on what we really believed made us special – secular morality and constitutional respect for the dignity of difference, unlike Pakistan – and still come out of it thinking we were intact.

Were we?

The pretence began in earnest after a brief period of genuinely shocked public soul-searching, which gave way to anger at the attacks on temples over the border. A cowed Indian Muslim community saw no alternative but to play along. We absorbed the horror of what we had done, and told ourselves new stories to cover the new reality and enshrine the muscular new Hindu rashtra that was being built. Those stories were key and in less than one generation, they have helped to create a new breed that I, for one, find hard to recognize.

In order to understand how this happened, consider the new research that is documenting the way in which the stories we read, hear and see change how we think and act. Neuroscientists and psychologists are increasingly reporting that the stories we absorb shape our thought processes, just as if they were a lived experience. Using modern technology like functional magnetic resonance imaging (fMRI) scanning of the brain, separate studies by Princeton University psychologists[8] and University of Southern California neuroscientists[9] put people in real-life situations – watching a Charlie Chaplin film, listening to moving true stories – and gauged the response. American science writer Elizabeth Svoboda describes the results in semi-layman-speak as follows:[10] 'Just when the speaker's brain lit up in the area of the insula – a region that governs empathy and moral sensibilities – the listeners' insulae lit up, too. Listeners and speakers also showed parallel activation of the temporoparietal junction, which helps us imagine other people's thoughts and emotions. In certain essential ways, then, stories help our brains map that of the storyteller.' She also reports a similar 2013 study at Amsterdam's Vrije Universiteit. 'Fiction readers who felt emotionally transported into a story scored higher on a scale of empathic concern one week after their reading experience.'

In recognition of the importance of yesterday's narrative to all our tomorrows, the American non-profit organization 'Facing History and Ourselves' has spent nearly forty years teaching school students in the US and increasingly in other parts of the world (Northern Ireland, South Africa, Israel, China, among other countries) that history is more than a list of dates and battles. 'It is the collective result of every individual's thoughts and actions.'[11] One of the ways that it does this is by encouraging the children to imagine themselves into the script. What would it have felt like, for instance, to be an ordinary German bystander while Kristallnacht, the Night of the Broken Glass, unfolded in all its ugly fury in November 1938? How would it feel to stand quietly by and watch synagogues being burned, windows smashed and Jewish shops looted? A Facing History class discussion typically works by inserting tomorrow's young adults into yesterday's events. So, for Kristallnacht, the children might be invited to imagine standing by while someone gets hurt or something bad is happening. This may prompt some of them to remember how bad they felt about doing nothing, while, say, a schoolmate was bullied, or something similar. Facing History students are anecdotally said to end the course more empathetic and civic-minded than those who never took it. But even if we don't yet have concrete numbers to prove this, it's impossible to discount the way a story can be used – or abused – to influence actions and outcomes.

But we know this already. From the way the Bhagavad Gita has been parsed, told and retold, for generations, each taking what it wills from the discourse between the troubled Pandava prince Arjun and Krishna, his guide and charioteer, on the Kurukshetra battlefield. To the BJP in 2015, the Gita appeared to be a tool to underline Hindu dominance of India, what with External Affairs Minister Sushma Swaraj controversially and unnecessarily calling for the text to be enshrined as India's 'national scripture'. To some freedom fighters, the Gita was a call to heroism. To Mahatma Gandhi, it was a 'spiritual dictionary', an instrument of liberation from the self, a manual that provided a gripping local story to spur on social and political action against British injustices. A wily strategist, the Mahatma used Krishna's exhortation – swadharma, the duty of every individual – to energize swadeshi, his version of what we call localism today.

It is a classic example of the power of a story from history that's still within living memory. For, whether we have read it or not, the values embedded within the story told in the Gita have come down to all of us by an unseen process of cultural osmosis. Every day, millions of Indians recite some fragment of the Gita. Every day, it is quoted by someone, somewhere. So we all know that it espouses the idea of doing one's duty or dharma. And we know that it elevates selfless action or karma yoga. That the BJP would seek to use the Gita to dominate and divide is probably not within the traditional definition of karma yoga, but then again, stories can be abused.

After 6 December 1992, when the Babri Masjid was destroyed, the collective contemporaneous story – as told or written, and that includes television, the print media and the wider national discourse – has largely absorbed the horror and shame of what we allowed to happen. Sans punishment, for the most part.[12] Sans cast-iron guarantees of 'never again'. Sans the accounts that might, like in a 'Facing History' class, give our children an empathetic understanding of what it might feel like to be an Indian Muslim watching the Babri mosque pulled down on television because 'your ancestors, you Babar ki aulad' had deliberately built it where the Hindus' revered Lord Ram was born. 'What did you expect?'

Some years ago, scientists of the University of Wisconsin–Madison and Brown University reported[13] that 'compassion can be cultivated with training and that greater altruistic behavior may emerge from increased engagement of neural systems implicated in understanding the suffering of other people, executive and emotional control, and reward processing'. Decoded, that seems to mean, you *can* teach people to care, to be less callous, perhaps even to cease to celebrate the crass mantras that have become the norm since 1992: Hindu might-is-right; my country-my-rules.

But then you have to turn the storytelling into less fable, more fact.

Unsurprisingly, the mantras have had other consequences – for art and culture and foreign policy. Today, we take a pallid stance on the plight of the Palestinians, in contrast to our early steadfast solidarity with their struggle for self-determination. This is not about what some call the 'encrusted' ideology of non-alignment, really a nullity today, but about principles of natural justice.

'CULT OF AUTHENTICITY'

Today, in an attempt at self-confident self-assertion, any intellectual exercise of any sort is turned over, carefully examined and sniffed all around, to see if it has what writer Vikram Chandra called 'the cult of authenticity'.[14] His memorable *Boston Review* essay of 2000 remains as valid, if not more so, today. At the outset, he describes a 1998 literary reading at the British Council in Delhi, featuring him, Sunil Khilnani and Ardeshir Vakil. Members asked each of them questions that somehow sought to undermine their work as posturing and consequently inauthentic. Khilnani was asked how he could live abroad and write about India; Vakil, if he went to such lengths to describe the preparation of bhelpuri in *Beach Boy* because he was writing for westerners who don't know what it is, and Chandra, if the titles of his stories ('Dharma', 'Artha', 'Kama') were meant only 'to signal Indianness in the West'.

As a consequence, Chandra became aware of 'the constant hum of this rhetoric, this anxiety about the anxiety of Indianness, this notion of a real reality that was being distorted by "Third World cosmopolitans", this fear of an all-devouring and all-distorting West'.

This aggressive attempt at self-preservation against an all-devouring, all-distorting West is now running in sync with peculiarly ludicrous self-aggrandizing claims[15] to the most impossible Hindu achievements while the world titters. How else to describe the assertion that the sages of Vedic times were so advanced they had the Pythagoras theorem long before the Greeks, knew algebra long before the Arabs and had jumbo aeroplanes, with forty small engines, no less, that could travel between the planets. And Prime Minister Modi himself has publicly wondered if the god Ganesh, with his elephant head and man's body, is proof positive of ancient Indian expertise at plastic surgery.

Indians have always taken great pride in the glories of their civilization but this particular bombastic trait seems new, to me and to many resident Indian observers as well. We were never as self-deprecating as our former colonial masters but as Manu Joseph recently wrote,[16] when he was in school 'the failure of India was unambiguous to all children. It was funny in the way death is funny sometimes. In fact, after the dumb Pakistani, the most popular jokes were about the dumb Indian. Only that generation and older would fully understand how amusing and odd the nationalism of the new middle class is.'

In a sense, the passing away on Republic Day 2015, of legendary cartoonist R.K. Laxman, underlined the definitive end of an era. Laxman created the befuddled 'Common Man' character, who was always peering around doors as ministers intoned at science and technology conventions by the light of a lantern that '... we expect to make still more brilliant progress ... in the coming years'. If the Common

Man was not morose, just silent and sharp-eyed, it was testimony to a certain lightness of being despite the great struggles under way in our poor populous country. Or at least an appreciable levity about what former *Times of India* editor Dileep Padgaonkar's salute to Laxman described as the Common Man's lot:[17] to bear silent witness to 'the squabbles, shenanigans and double-speak of the nation's movers and shakers'.

There had to be a magnificent sense of goodwill – towards ourselves, most importantly – to endure the fact that millions of ordinary Indians struggled through every single day because of the babus, the red tape, the eternal ghoos (bribe), while our leaders claimed so much, did so little, all with such self-regarding zeal. The Common Man was in on the national joke and chimed with the spirit of the times. But that age of gentle, keen-eyed humour was over, long before Laxman's death, at ninety-three.

It had given way to a different sort of hard-edged stand-up and spoof, which too reflects the times and is an answer of sorts to the deadly serious 'nationalism of the new middle-class'. This nationalistic fervour is hard to deal with and it might be admirable if it limited itself to nation building – at whatever cost to oneself, in terms of paying the right amount of tax and any appropriate traffic violation fines, rather than taking out opinions, and those who express them. Especially from NRIs, Khilnani or anyone else, who dares to deviate from the India-rising, Jai Ho script. Aam NRIs, without Nobel Prizes and Hall of Fame credentials, are fair game if they presume to say anything negative or even mildly questioning of the way things are in the motherland.

And it all goes particularly sour when celebrity 'Indian-born' people decline to be co-opted by the groupthink. After Indian-born American-British scientist Venkataraman Ramakrishnan won the 2009 Nobel Prize in chemistry, and famously said it was entirely unimportant that he was of Indian origin, 'we are all human beings, and our nationality is simply an accident of birth',[18] the shock was followed by attempts to belittle him. Journalist Kumkum Chadha thundered in a *Hindustan Times* blog[19] that she had always believed 'that the greatest damage to India is done by its own countrymen. I am witness to several Indians settled abroad who take the lead in running down their own country in the presence of foreigners. They start the country-mockery before others would venture or dare to. The pride in India and the phenomenon of being a proud Indian is a recent one. Before that Indians were ashamed of being seen or referred to as Indians and did everything possible to conceal their identity and origin. I sense Ramakrishnan's contempt towards Indians stems from this mindset.' There was other caterwauling by others, in the same vein.[20]

It's hard to be sure if Mr Ramakrishnan was displaying 'contempt towards Indians' or restating the universality of the human family (which Mahatma Gandhi would have recognized). But there is some truth in Kumkum Chadha's assertion: 'The pride in India and the phenomenon of being a proud Indian is a recent one.' Warts and all. Except that you're not allowed to mention or even notice the warts if you're part of the India Club. Prickliness is not, of course, exclusive to India and Indians. But the blanket requirement – abandon thought, all ye who want to be part of the fraternity – is decidedly unusual for a people with so many strengths.

Who, or what, is the 'new' India then? After living all over the world, it is diverting to consider the extent to which India is becoming more like the rest of the world in so many ways, and so much less like itself and entirely distinct from its early idealized idea of itself.

So here goes.

Now, we are more like the French in our cultural snobbery, but the glories, alas, are receding ever further into the past. We don't spend much money or thought on efforts to protect or subsidize our cultural heritage and industries and boost artistic creativity.

We are more like the Americans in the insistence on our exceptionalism.

We are becoming more like Israel at least in terms of some efforts to become a theocracy.

But we are not sufficiently like the magnificently efficient Germans.

We are not like the English (hallelujah, we're not bad cooks) in that we lack that disarming ability to laugh at ourselves.

But worst of all, we're not even like the Pakistanis, who have at least stuck by the guiding religious principle of their nationhood.

There is one excruciatingly uncomfortable fact of knowing that the world knows we know: we aren't what exactly who we say we are. We are forced to dissemble in full view of everybody. Consider the Ministry of External Affairs' eight-minute long video,[21] released after Barack Obama became the only American president to visit India twice during his tenure, as well as the first to be chief guest at the Republic Day parade. It was a glitzy product – good for the most part and recording the American president's verdict on Prime Minister Modi: 'He's tough ... he has style.'

But, it did not go unnoticed, not least by the world's press,[22] that the video was carefully edited to remove Mr Obama's comment on his final day in Delhi, that 'India will succeed as long as it's not splintered along religious lines'. That was clearly meant to convey an important message: The world is reassured only when India lives up to the ideal of religious freedom originally envisioned by those who freed it from colonial rule.

That this had to be removed from the official narrative only underlines the power of the story.

NOTES

1 Simon Jenkins, columnist with *The Guardian* and former editor, *The Times*, London, once told me an amusing story that illustrated different places' different notions of belongingness. After a row broke out over his rather non-PC comments on Birmingham in the English Midlands, he was reviled by the city's politicians as an out-and-out Londoner with no idea of what he spoke and no right to say it anyway.

But when he revealed that he was born in Birmingham, the city's worthies turned off the ire. 'Why didn't you say so before,' they told him, 'you're one of us.'

2 From Deirdre Bair's 1995 biography of the Cuban American polyamorist writer. She says that Nin described her two simultaneous marriages as a 'bicoastal trapeze' act. She wrote that '[Anaïs] would set up these elaborate façades in Los Angeles and in New York, but it became so complicated that she had to create something she called the lie box. She had this absolutely enormous purse and in the purse she had two sets of checkbooks. One said Anaïs Guiler for New York and another said Anaïs Pole for Los Angeles. She had prescription bottles from California doctors and New York doctors with the two different names. And she had a collection of file cards. And she said, "I tell so many lies I have to write them down and keep them in the lie box so I can keep them straight."'

3 In August 1999, Prince Philip, husband of the British Queen, was touring a high-tech electronics company on the outskirts of Edinburgh, when he spotted a fuse box that looked less sophisticated than other state-of-the-art equipment in the plant. 'It looks as though it was put in by an Indian,' he said.

4 *Groundwork of the Metaphysic of Morals*, published 1785, was Immanuel Kant's first major work on moral philosophy. He argued that with the exception of the good will, all goods are qualified. For example, wealth can be good if it is used for human welfare, but it can be disastrous if a corrupt mind is behind it. We often take intelligence to be good, but would not take the intelligence of an evil genius to be good. The good will, by contrast, is good in itself. It cannot be qualified by what it effects or accomplishes. Or doesn't.

5 On its website, the BJP's account of L.K. Advani's 1990 rathyatra promises that the 'pilgrimage' will only end when the Babri mosque destruction is taken to its logical conclusion, a temple for the infant Lord Rama at the place of his birth. 'Today, the BJP is the largest political party in the country, thanks to the journey that began from Somnath during the Navaratri of 1990. The procession that began with

a handful of nationalists led by an uncompromising nationalist is today a roaring stream of nationalist fervour. The pilgrimage will be over the day Ram Lalla finds his rightful place in a temple commemorating the sacred site of his birth.' http://www.bjp.org/leadership/shri-lk-advani/ yatras/?u=ram-rath-yatra

6   Twenty days after L.K. Advani's rathyatra began, *India Today* reported the ecstatic scenes along the way: 'Hindutva supporters rang temple bells, beat thalis and shouted slogans to welcome the rath. Some smeared the rath with a tilak and smeared the dust from its wheels on their forehead ... Although in his autobiography, *My Country My Life*, Advani calls this rathyatra, "an exhilarating period in my political life", it was much more than that. It whipped up a strong Hindu fervor ...' http://indiatoday.intoday.in/story/1990 L.K.+Advani%27s+rath+ yatra:+Chariot+of+fire/1/76389.html

7   In a guest post dated 18 March 2014, for Kafila, a blog that describes itself as 'a collaborative practice of radical political and media critique, and an engagement with the present', Jawaharlal Nehru University PhD scholar Raoof Mir wrote about the 'periodic tests of loyalty' to which Indian Muslims are subjected. Just days before, a group of students of the Swami Vivekananda Subharti University in Uttar Pradesh had been suspended for cheering Pakistan's victory over India in a nail-biting finish to the Asia Cup. Mr Mir noted the communal tensions that have consistently marked India–Pakistan cricket face-offs – the 1999 and 2003 World Cups. And he recalls the 2007 Hindi movie *Bheja Fry*'s portrayal of Asif Merchant, an Indian Muslim who supports the Pakistan cricket team over the Indian cricket team. He 'is shown as a comical, hideous, perfidious character with loyalties to Pakistan despite living in India – taunted with "yahan ke khaate ho, aur wahan ke gaateho"(you eat off India but sing the praises of Pakistan).'

8   Uri Hasson, an assistant professor in Princeton's Department of Psychology and the Princeton Neuroscience Institute, is studying the underlying neural mechanisms of the processes that allow the brain to integrate information over time using non-traditional experiments that mimic real-life situations. In 2010, for instance, a student was

asked to tell an unrehearsed fifteen-minute story about one of her high-school proms – a disastrous experience involving two suitors, a fistfight and a car accident – while her brain was scanned. Then twelve other study participants were scanned via fMRI while listening to a recording of the story. The results showed that not only did all of the listeners show similar brain activity during the story, but the speaker and the listeners also had very similar brain activity as well, despite the fact that one person was producing language and the others were comprehending it. This brain coupling or 'mind meld' was published in the *Proceedings of the National Academy of Sciences* journal in 2010.

9   'Neural Correlates of Admiration and Compassion', by Mary Helen Immordino-Yang, Andrea McColl, Hanna Damasio and Antonio Damasio appeared in the *Proceedings of the National Academy of Sciences* in April 2009. It reported the results of their fMRI experiment, in which participants were exposed to narratives based on true stories designed to evoke admiration and compassion in four distinct categories: admiration for virtue, admiration for skill, compassion for social/psychological pain, and compassion for physical pain. The brain scans showed a fierce identification with the characters in the stories and that the emotion-driven responses started in the brain stem, which governs physical functions, such as digestion and heartbeat.

10   In 'The Power of Story', *Aeon* magazine, January 2015, Elizabeth Svoboda writes: 'Across time and culture, stories have been agents of personal transformation – in part because they change our brains.' Presumably that includes 'good' narratives and 'bad' ones like hate speech or accounts that stress racial or cultural superiority.

11   Facing History and Ourselves started in Brookline, Massachusetts, as a history class about the ideas and events that led to the Holocaust. Using an approach that went beyond the textbook and employed discussion, character exploration, primary source material, and group exercises instead, its 'students saw the tragic events from every perspective. In the process, they came to understand that history is the collective result of every individual's thoughts and actions. They

learned not only history, but also the critical thinking skills required to make good choices.' With a physical and/or virtual presence in many countries, the organization says its mission is to enable 'transformative dialogue' and foster empathy and reflection. 'Through rigorous investigation of the events that led to the Holocaust and other recent examples of genocide and mass violence, students in a Facing History class learn to choose knowledge over misinformation, compassion over prejudice or bullying, and participation over indifference or resignation. It's active rather than passive learning.'

12   On 6 December 2014, twenty-two years after the mosque was demolished, the Pakistani press reported that members of the All India Babri Masjid Rebuilding Committee and the All India Muslim Unity Front had protested in Delhi and urged the Supreme Court of India to pronounce on the dispute as soon as possible. They said that by 'demolishing the Babri Masjid in 1992, several organizations violated the Constitution, judiciary, law and order and harmed the secular character of India on international level'. Meanwhile, Digvijaya Singh, general secretary of the Congress party, now in Opposition, tweeted that the demolition 'unleashed polarization in Indian politics. The accused must be punished.' http://www.thenews.com.pk/Todays-News-1-288769-Punish-those-responsible-for-demolishing-Babri-Masjid

13   'Compassion Training Alters Altruism and Neural Responses to Suffering' was published in *Psychological Science*, a journal of the Association for Psychological Science.

14   Chandra suggests that it is resident non-Indians (ethnically Indian but far removed from the realities of life in India) rather than non-resident Indians who are the problem. 'And the devil is of course within ourselves: the most vociferously anti-Western crusaders I meet are inevitably the ones who are most hybrid. It is these comfortably situated citizens, these Resident Non-Indians, who, beset by a consciousness of their own isolation from "Real India", feel an overpowering nostalgia for an Indianness that never was, for a mythical, paradisaical lost garden of cultural and spiritual unity.'

http://www.bostonreview.net/vikram-chandra-the-cult-of-authenticity

15 At the Indian Science Congress in January 2015, Captain Anand J. Bodas, the retired principal of a pilot training facility, said the world's first plane was invented by Maharishi Bharadwaj and India's science and technology minister Harsh Vardhan claimed credit on behalf of the sages for the Pythagorean theorem and algebra. It drew criticism from D. Raghunandan, president of the All India People's Scientific Network, who said, 'We are giving a young, aspirational generation a wrong idea of science. And this is why nobody takes Indian scientists seriously.'

16 'Is seeking pride from history a response to shame?', Manu Joseph, *Hindustan Times*, 15 December 2014.

17 'No more Laxman rekhas: Common Man orphaned, but legacy stays', by Dileep Padgaonkar, *The Times of India*, 27 January 2015.

18 In an email interview with PTI, soon after the prize was announced, Venkataraman Ramakrishnan said, 'All sorts of people from India have been writing to me and clogging up my email box. It takes me an hour or two to just remove their mails. Do these people have no consideration? It is OK to take pride in the event but why bother me ... There are also people who have never ever bothered to be in touch with me for decades who feel the urge to connect. I find this strange ...'

19 A Nobel laureate's reaction to adulation, 17 November 2009. http://blogs.hindustantimes.com/just-people/2009/11/17/are-we-still-proud-of-him/

20 'Hey, Venkatraman Ramakrishnan, you've NOT got mail', Farzana Versey, 14 October 2009. 'One day, when the Western press asks you about anything on India, and they just might – about its foreign policy, its poverty, its global leap – please do not give your opinion. Even though you may be well-read, speak as a foreigner, not as one who knows. Coz, although you might remember the ground as you learned to crawl here, you don't know the ground realities.' http://farzana-versey.blogspot.com/2009/10/hey-venkatraman-ramakrishnan-youve-not.html

21   http://www.mea.gov.in/

22   'Watch: What's missing from India's glitzy video of Obama's visit', *The Washington Post*, 29 January 2015. The article noted: 'While the MEA might like to forget it, Obama's speech in Delhi was perhaps his most high profile ...'

It also referred to the *Wall Street Journal* article on the same subject, 'Watch India's Airbrushed Version of Obama Visit'.